M000316564

seeing the
invisible

DESTINY IMAGE BOOKS BY DON NORI, SR.

seeing the
invisible

90 Days of Experiencing the Passion,
Presence, & Purpose of God

Don Nori, Sr. & Dr. Thom Gardner

DESTINY IMAGE® PUBLISHERS, INC.

P.O. Box 310, Shippensburg, PA 17257-0310

"Promoting Inspired Lives."

This book and all other Destiny Image and Destiny Image Fiction books are available at Christian bookstores and distributors worldwide.

Cover design by Eileen Rockwell
Interior design by Terry Clifton

For more information on foreign distributors, call 717-532-3040.
Reach us on the Internet: www.destinyimage.com.

ISBN 13 TP: 978-0-7684-4724-8
ISBN 13 eBook: 978-0-7684-4725-5
ISBN 13 HC: 978-0-7684-4724-8
ISBN 13 LP: 978-0-7684-4726-2

For Worldwide Distribution, Printed in the U.S.A.
1 2 3 4 5 6 7 8 / 23 22 21 20 19

CONTENTS

EDITOR'S INTRODUCTION

A comment made by friends of Don Nori was that he could *see* what others could not *see*—*Seeing the Invisible*. That applied both in Don's intimate connection with God and also with people. Don had the unusual ability to then make his connection with God visible to people, expressing deep truth in common words and through everyday life. Don's great passion was to see the Christ whom he loved take up His abiding place in the hearts of His people. The Jesus whom Don loved and who loved Don could not be contained in tradition or God-theories; He was alive and living through the lives of common people.

Don was not shy about sharing the realities of his own journey with Jesus. As I read through the words of his many books, his journey with Jesus was obvious. I was one of Don's close friends for more than thirty-five years and was a first-hand witness of his journey with its highs and lows. Regardless of life's perceived potholes along the way, Don's face was ever set on seeing Jesus and making Him visible to common folks. Don's writings represent a relentless pursuit of the person of Jesus Christ.

This is where you, the reader, come in. This book sets forth a 90-day journey with God in three sections that represent themes of Don's teaching through the years. I have titled the sections the *passion*, the *Presence*, and the *purpose*, which reflects Don's focus for much of his writing. Each devotion features a quotation from one of Don's books with care to preserve his words. (Don was an excellent wordsmith who had a particular rhythm and cadence in his writing.) Each devotion has a singular focus represented by a headline at the beginning of the devotion. These short and focused devotions are then accompanied by related Scriptures that help to amplify and provide further evidence supporting the theme of that devotion.

APPROACHING THE DEVOTION

Each devotional article has three sections—*read, reflect, respond*. They will be labeled in each article. The reader is encouraged to *read* the devotional then the scriptures that follow. Each devotion includes a summary statement, an encouragement, and also a prompt for journaling. I encourage you to *reflect* on the devotion and Scriptures and write what comes to your heart. Words, thoughts, images will stand out along the way as the Holy Spirit applies His highlighter to the devotion. The journaling prompt is meant to be a guideline for the reader's personal reflection of the devotion, not a guardrail. Use the journaling spaces to grow and *respond* on your own journey with God to *make the invisible visible.*

As you begin each devotion, take a few moments to focus yourself in a quiet place with Jesus. Read the words slowly and reflectively. The devotions are not lengthy, so you may want to savor the words and reflect throughout the day. One of Don's oft-used invitations from Jesus was "Come to Me." Allow yourself to respond to Jesus' kind invitation through the devotional article. Read the devotional article and the accompanying Scriptures, slowly savoring the words. As you read, notice words or feelings that stand out to you. Take time to soak in the words and images that surface to your attention. Don't try to analyze or define the words as much as simply noticing or attending them.

As you journal, you may want to highlight, circle, or write out the words that arise so that you can carry them with you for the day. These words stood out to you for a reason. Let them do their work in you throughout the day. You will notice at the end of your journal entry that there is a space with the heading: "How will I live these truths today?" In this space write down a few practical thoughts to express what your spirit is learning. Information without practical application is of little value in the journey. Jesus said, "Go and do likewise."

ON A PERSONAL NOTE

As I was reading through Don's books and reflecting on Don's words, I could hear his voice once more—a voice that sat across from me at the table through many breakfasts and lunches. I could remember Don's times with his sons who meant everything to him. This book was compiled from the writings of my buddy of many years. As I have gathered these words together, I felt the Presence of God with me. I've listened to each devotional thought to share my friend's voice with you. These words are of eternal scope and value.

I miss my friend Don, as I am sure his other many friends do. As I read through Don's books again I have found that many of Don's words shaped my own walk with Christ. Now as you walk the footsteps of Don's journey into the heart of Jesus Christ, you also will be shaped by his words. Allow yourself to be gathered into the Presence of Jesus and write a new chapter in your own journey. It is my prayer that you will *experience the passion*, learn to *live in the Presence*, and *find your ultimate purpose in God*. With each step of this journey, you will be transformed into the dwelling place of Christ, and through your life many will be *Seeing the Invisible*.

Part One

EXPERIENCING THE PASSION OF GOD

IT'S A NEW DAY IN GOD'S LOVE

READ

Today is a new day full of hope and promise, because God wants to show His love for you. God wants you to experience His love and enjoy it every day. Today marks the end of your search for His love and the beginning of the answer you have hoped and prayed for as long as you can remember—God knows all your needs. He cares for you—the real you. It doesn't matter to Him who society or culture says you are. You could be the president of the United States, a movie star, a businessperson, a stay-at-home mom, a student, or a youngster. You could be married, single, or divorced. You may be unemployed. You may be black, white, or brown. God sees your heart and knows everything you need. He sees us all as His children, and He loves, blesses, and cares for all of us equally. The first thing all people need to acknowledge is that the emptiness deep down inside can only be filled with God's love (*How to Find God's Love*, 18).

Further Evidence

> *But each day the Lord pours his unfailing love upon me, and through each night I sing his songs, praying to God who gives me life* (Psalm 42:8).

> *The faithful love of the Lord never ends! His mercies never cease. Great is his faithfulness; his mercies begin afresh each morning* (Lamentations 3:22-23).

> *Seek the Kingdom of God above all else, and live righteously, and he will give you everything you need. So don't worry about tomorrow, for tomorrow will bring its own worries. Today's trouble is enough for today* (Matthew 6:33-34).

REFLECT: SEEING THE INVISIBLE

(Remember to circle, underline, or otherwise highlight any words or images that stand out to you in the devotional or the related Scriptures.)

Are there places of emptiness in your heart and life today? Invite God to fill those empty places in your heart and life. It's a new day!

RESPOND

Considering the devotional and the scriptures above, take time to sit in a quiet place with Jesus and journal what God's passionate love means to you personally.

How will I make this visible through my life today?

8/20/19

God's Passionate love means everything to me. It's the most important thing in the world to me & I want to love exactly the same way as God does. I will make this visible through my life today by putting God's word in my heart, meditating on the word & being a doer of the word. Also by staying humble, walking in the spirit, renewing my mind, sharing the love of God with others as much as I can.

2

True Love Is the Passion and the Very Nature of God

READ

Love simply comes, often undetected even by the one overtaken by its mysterious powers. True love. The lonely covet its reality. The arrogant flaunt its Presence. The ignorant snub its wonder. It is as illogical as anything can be. It is hopeless to describe it and folly to shun it. The greatest philosophers have sought to define it. Religion has tried to buy it. Many have tried to elude it. Love is as hopeless to understand as it is impossible to deny. Yet reason and logic are helpless against love, for it is a most formidable foe of the mundane and the average. True love, you see, dares to go places where reason cannot tread. Love sees realities about which philosophy can only hope to dimly speculate. True love knows what tradition can only distantly remember. True love draws the least lovable. It can make anyone a hero. True love is the sustaining power of the universe itself, yet is so lovely that it abides fully in the hearts of those foolish enough to respond to its rapturous invitation to come (*Romancing the Divine*, 5).

Further Evidence

> *Yahweh! The Lord! The God of compassion and mercy! I am slow to anger and filled with unfailing love and faithfulness* (Exodus 34:6).

> *O Lord, God of Israel, there is no God like you in all of heaven and earth. You keep your covenant and show unfailing love to all who walk before you in wholehearted devotion* (2 Chronicles 6:14).

> *How precious is your unfailing love, O God! All humanity finds shelter in the shadow of your wings* (Psalm 36:7).

REFLECT: SEEING THE INVISIBLE

(Remember to circle, underline, or otherwise highlight any words or images that stand out to you in the devotional or the related Scriptures. Include them in your journaling response.)

The love of God defies all reason. It's not based on what you do but who you are as beloved children of God. You have only to accept it.

RESPOND

Settle yourself in the quiet Presence of Jesus to journal about what it means to be the beloved child of God.

How will I make this visible through my life today?

3

GOD IS LOVE!

READ

Finding God's love is actually finding God Himself. Finding God's love is finding a personal friendship with a personal God. Finding His love is finding Him closely and intimately involved with your day-to-day activities and circumstances. Finding God's love is finding healing and forgiveness of sins. It means finding freedom from bitterness and hatred. It's finding God's strength to walk away from sins and habits that have kept you a prisoner for too many years. Finding God's love means finding true reality and true life. Finding God's love is finding Him through Jesus Christ. Jesus is God's answer for the world. As you can see, finding God's love is far more than a prayer, far more than what you do and don't do. It is the fulfillment of your heart's desire for real friendship with God. Nothing else in the world can fill that God-shaped emptiness within (*How to Find God's Love*, 53).

Further Evidence

Dear friends, let us continue to love one another, for love comes from God. Anyone who loves is a child of God and knows God. But anyone who does not love does not know God, for God is love. God showed how much he loved us by sending his one and only Son into the world so that we might have eternal life through him. This is real love— not that we loved God, but that he loved us and sent his Son as a sacrifice to take away our sins (1 John 4:7-10).

REFLECT: SEEING THE INVISIBLE

(Remember to circle, underline, or otherwise highlight any words or images that stand out to you in the devotional or the related Scriptures. Include them in your journaling response.)

All of us have a longing emptiness in our hearts that can only be filled with God's love. What kinds of things have you done to try to fill that emptiness with something else?

RESPOND

Sit in a quiet place with Jesus and ask Him to fill those empty places with His love. Journal your experience.

How will I make this visible through my life today?

....

....

....

God Is Love!

4

GOD'S LOVE IS REAL!

READ

God is a personal God whose greatest joy is having us as friends. In the beginning of time, God created Adam and Eve because He wanted someone to talk to. He loved the people He had created and intended them to live with Him in the Garden of Eden forever. God's love stands ready to set us free from the hurt and pain we have suffered or are suffering now. Finding God's love is not just a free ticket to a far-away Heaven someday. It does not mean finding mediocre answers and lame excuses. His love is real. It is far more than most of humankind has ever imagined. When God's love is found, the relationship that God had with Adam is restored to you. The friendship and joy of fellowship is as dynamic for us as it was for Adam and Eve. God is not interested in just filling up Heaven (*How to Find God's Love* 26, 54).

Further Evidence

> *There is no greater love than to lay down one's life for one's friends. You are my friends if you do what I*

command. I no longer call you slaves, because a master doesn't confide in his slaves. Now you are my friends, since I have told you everything the Father told me (John 15:13-15).

And so it happened just as the Scriptures say: "Abraham believed God, and God counted him as righteous because of his faith." He was even called the friend of God (James 2:23).

I have told you all this so that you may have peace in me. Here on earth you will have many trials and sorrows. But take heart, because I have overcome the world (John 16:33).

REFLECT: SEEING THE INVISIBLE

(Remember to circle, underline, or otherwise highlight any words or images that stand out to you in the devotional or the related Scriptures. Include them in your journaling response.)

God wants to walk with you as a friends. Share your life with God today as you might with a friend. Talk to Him, share your heart with Him, listen to Him.

RESPOND

Sit quietly with Jesus and journal your conversation with Him.

How will I make this visible through my life today?

5

WE ARE SECURE IN THE ARMS OF GOD'S LOVE

READ

When God's love came bursting into my heart, I found that there was more, much more. To my great delight, I could feel Him close to me. Deep in my heart, I could hear Him speak to me. There was a peace and an assurance that came over me that I experience even to this day. As time went on and I discovered more about God's love and the dream He dreamt for me, my joy grew. I began to understand that I indeed had a reason to live! Although all of my problems remained, now I had God. He would help me! There is no greater place of contentment and security than in His arms (*How to Find God's Love*, 39).

Further Evidence

> *The eternal God is a dwelling place, and underneath are the everlasting arms* (Deuteronomy 33:27 NASB).

You made all the delicate, inner parts of my body and knit me together in my mother's womb. Thank you for making me so wonderfully complex! Your workmanship is marvelous—how well I know it (Psalm 139:13-14).

He will feed his flock like a shepherd. He will carry the lambs in his arms, holding them close to his heart. He will gently lead the mother sheep with their young (Isaiah 40:11).

I am the good shepherd. The good shepherd sacrifices his life for the sheep (John 10:11).

REFLECT: SEEING THE INVISIBLE

(Remember to circle, underline, or otherwise highlight any words or images that stand out to you in the devotional or the related Scriptures. Include them in your journaling response.)

Just as you long to be close to God, He longs to be close to you. Allow yourself to be in the secure arms of the Shepherd.

RESPOND

Quietly focus on the enfolding Presence on the Shepherd and journal your feelings here.

How will I make this visible through my life today?

....

....

....

6

GOD'S LOVE FREES US FROM LIES WE BELIEVE ABOUT OURSELVES

READ

Everything changed at that moment! I rejoiced as well as rested in the knowledge that I was born for a purpose. I knew that there was a destiny for me in God. It didn't matter where I worked or where I lived. God had a plan for me and I was sure of it. I had found God's love. The whole world looked entirely different than it did before. Even how I looked at myself was different. I had *found* God's love. I realized I had worth. I had value, really. After all, if the God of all creation took a personal interest in me and if He had a personal love for me, how could I keep thinking the same old depressing thoughts? How could I believe the same old lies? How could I feel so worthless if God Almighty loved me? It felt so great to be truly free (*How to Find God's Love*, 40).

Further Evidence

> *The Spirit of the Lord is upon me, for he has anointed me to bring Good News to the poor. He has sent me to*

proclaim that captives will be released, that the blind will see, that the oppressed will be set free, and that the time of the Lord's favor has come. (Luke 4:18-19).

For when we died with Christ we were set free from the power of sin (Romans 6:7).

This means that anyone who belongs to Christ has become a new person. The old life is gone; a new life has begun! (2 Corinthians 5:17)

REFLECT: SEEING THE INVISIBLE

(Remember to circle, underline, or otherwise highlight any words or images that stand out to you in the devotional or the related Scriptures. Include them in your journaling response.)

How do you see yourself? Look at yourself today from the perspective of God's love for you. How does your life look different to you?

RESPOND

Sit quietly with Jesus and journal about your unshackled life wrapped in the love of God.

How will I make this visible through my life today?

7

YOU ARE GOD'S GREATEST JOY!

READ

Not many people really think about God from this perspective. Most are concerned only with trying to create and satisfy their own desires and pleasures. Nevertheless, there is joy that God considers His greatest! That "greatest joy" is *you*. God is not too busy keeping the planets in orbit. He is not too busy trying to end wars and famine. He's not too busy counting stars or creating new ones. He doesn't have to find the time to hear your prayer or "squeeze in" your requests between major global events. You are not His hobby. He doesn't only answer you on weekends or His days off. You are not His sideline interest. You are His greatest joy! As a husband enjoys the love of his wife, so God enjoys your love. God is a personal God whose greatest joy is having us as friends. God wants *you* to have His love and joy deep in your heart—forever (*How to Find God's Love*, 26-27).

Further Evidence

> *Because you are my helper, I sing for joy in the shadow of your wings* (Psalm 63:7).

> *Fixing our eyes on Jesus, the author and perfecter of faith, who for the joy set before Him endured the cross, despising the shame, and has sat down at the right hand of the throne of God* (Hebrews 12:2 NASB).

> *These things I have spoken to you so that My joy may be in you, and that your joy may be made full* (John 15:11 NASB).

REFLECT: SEEING THE INVISIBLE

(Remember to circle, underline, or otherwise highlight any words or images that stand out to you in the devotional or the related Scriptures. Include them in your journaling response.)

God is never too busy for you; you are not interrupting something more important with your prayers of communication with Him. You are His joy today!

RESPOND

While sitting in a quiet place with Jesus, journal your thoughts about bringing joy to the heart of God. You are the joy set before Jesus!

How will I make this visible through my life today?

8

LOVE SETS US FREE!

READ

When you give your heart to Jesus, you are freed from your past. You are a brand-new person; all the old stuff passes away and you begin a whole new life. It does not matter what others say about you or think about you. When you find God's love, you belong to Him. You alone are the judge. Others cannot separate you from Him. There was such power when God raised Jesus from the dead that the devil's power over humankind was forever crushed. If we will respond to God's love, we can experience the same power that raised Jesus Christ from the dead. This is really true. Countless millions experience this resurrection power every single day. You can, too (*How to Find God's Love*, 63).

Further Evidence

So if the Son makes you free, you will be free indeed (John 8:36 NASB).

Therefore if anyone is in Christ, he is a new creature; the old things passed away; behold, new things have come (2 Corinthians 5:17 NASB).

So Christ has truly set us free. Now make sure that you stay free, and don't get tied up again in slavery to the law (Galatians 5:1).

REFLECT: SEEING THE INVISIBLE

(Remember to circle, underline, or otherwise highlight any words or images that stand out to you in the devotional or the related Scriptures. Include them in your journaling response.)

Do you hang on to old stuff in your life—hurts, disappointments, sins, and more? Surrender anything you are hauling behind you and experience the freedom Christ won for you. Live free!

RESPOND

Sit quietly with Jesus and ask Him what He wants you to leave behind in order to enjoy freedom with Him.

How will I make this visible through my life today?

....

....

....

....

....

9

GOD'S LOVE OVERWHELMS MY SIN

READ

Unless I can come to God under His terms, I will not experience His love. I must be cleansed (by the blood of Christ) so that I can draw near to Him and begin to experience the full impact of His love. We must not confuse our own feelings with what God has said. It is also true that we should not confuse the feelings of others with what God has said. Remember that we are harder on ourselves than God is. We and others are less likely to forgive. But God's love is always moved, motivated by, and forever under the influence of His overwhelming love for us individually. He forgives us. Period. There is no human being who has committed too many sins for God to forgive. There is no stain of sin too hard for Him to wash away. His will is for all people to experience His love (*How to Find God's Love*, 78-79).

Further Evidence

> *"For I know the plans I have for you," says the Lord. "They are plans for good and not for disaster, to give you a future and a hope"* (Jeremiah 29:11).

> *Then Jesus said, "Come to me, all of you who are weary and carry heavy burdens, and I will give you rest. Take my yoke upon you. Let me teach you, because I am humble and gentle at heart, and you will find rest for your souls. For my yoke is easy to bear, and the burden I give you is light"* (Matthew 11:28-30).

> *Now on the last day, the great day of the feast, Jesus stood and cried out, saying, "If anyone is thirsty, let him come to Me and drink. He who believes in Me, as the Scripture said, 'From his innermost being will flow rivers of living water'"* (John 7:37-38 NASB).

REFLECT: SEEING THE INVISIBLE

(Remember to circle, underline, or otherwise highlight any words or images that stand out to you in the devotional or the related Scriptures. Include them in your journaling response.)

Sometimes you are hard on yourself. Remember that you come to God through grace alone through Jesus Christ. Be aware today of the words you say about yourself.

RESPOND

Quiet yourself with Jesus and share with Him where you have tried to do life on your own. Journal your conversation here.

How will I make this visible through my life today?

....

....

....

....

....

....

....

....

....

....

....

....

....

....

....

....

....

....

10

In Love, Both Man and God Find True Rest

Read

Let's admit it; we all want to have God's love in our lives. Most of us want to know that we are pleasing God daily. But it is also true that most of us do not think that we please Him or that there is anything we can do to be pleasing to Him every day. We look to books for help. At the end of the day, the books that are usually the most popular are the ones that seem to be the most helpful to us. These books are all part of our journey to the Love Shack (*abiding in the love of God*)— the place of uncontested favor and acceptance. It is the place where mere mortals can rest in the peace and assurance that they are certainly accepted in the Lord and gathered into His family for blessing, care, favor, protection, and strength. The Love Shack is the place where destiny is discovered and hope is revived. Of all the places in time or out of time, in this dimension or any other, the Love Shack is the place where we can completely rest in His love. The Love Shack is where God rests too (*Love Shack*, 37).

Further Evidence

> *And He said, "My presence shall go with you, and I will give you rest"* (Exodus 33:14 NASB).

> *Be still, and know that I am God!* (Psalm 46:10)

> *Then Jesus said, "Let's go off by ourselves to a quiet place and rest awhile"* (Mark 6:31).

> *I have loved you even as the Father has loved me. Remain in my love* (John 15:9).

REFLECT: SEEING THE INVISIBLE

(Remember to circle, underline, or otherwise highlight any words or images that stand out to you in the devotional or the related Scriptures. Include them in your journaling response.)

We all long to be loved and accepted by God unconditionally. Today is the day to accept the grace of God's love. Accept the free gift of God's love for you simply for being you.

RESPOND

Quietly consider the devotional and the Sscriptures above. What do you hear as you rest with Jesus?

How will I make this visible through my life today?

....

....

11

GOD'S LOVE TRULY IS NOT CONDITIONALLY UNCONDITIONAL

READ

My prayers have changed significantly over the years. I am no longer the uncertain beggar trying to convince God of my worthiness to be blessed. I do not try to convince Him I am worthy to love. I am not. I know it, He knows it, and He laughs, for His love is "just because." He loves—no explanation needed. He loves, period. If there is any convincing to be done, it is in my need to accept His incredible, unconditional love for me. Oh, I know that we are taught about His unconditional love, but religion always seems to give it conditions. What? How can unconditional love have conditions? This is just one of religion's many outrageous oxymorons. Conditional unconditional love is a conundrum that will never find its way into the resting place of the Love Shack, for it opposes everything for which Jesus gave Himself (*Love Shack*, 39-40).

Further Evidence

> *Let your unfailing love surround us, Lord, for our hope is in you alone* (Psalm 33:22).

> *But God is so rich in mercy, and he loved us so much, that even though we were dead because of our sins, he gave us life when he raised Christ from the dead. (It is only by God's grace that you have been saved!)* (Ephesians 2:4-5)

> *Dear friends, let us continue to love one another, for love comes from God. Anyone who loves is a child of God and knows God. But anyone who does not love does not know God, for God is love. God showed how much he loved us by sending his one and only Son into the world so that we might have eternal life through him* (1 John 4:7-9).

REFLECT: SEEING THE INVISIBLE

(Remember to circle, underline, or otherwise highlight any words or images that stand out to you in the devotional or the related Scriptures. Include them in your journaling response.)

What conditions have you imposed on God's unconditional love for you? You can rest in the reality of God's love for you without adding further requirements.

RESPOND

As you sit quietly with Jesus, ask Him to reveal conditions you have added to His unconditional love for you. Journal your responses here.

How will I make this visible through my life today?

....

....

....

....

....

....

....

....

....

....

....

....

....

....

....

....

....

....

12

In Love We Move from Beggars to Lovers of God

Read

I no longer counsel the Lord in my prayers. I have ceased to clutter the spiritual air with personal opinions and directives. He has convinced me that I can trust Him. He has convinced me that He always has my best interests at heart. My prayer times have changed from the beggar to the lover. Now my conversations with Him are much like the conversations I have with my wife. Cathy and I know that we can trust each other. I don't have to worry or wonder about her fulfilling her daily responsibilities any more than she has to worry about me fulfilling mine. We do not remind each other of the so-called mundane things of everyday life that we do in response to our love for each other. Love constrains us to do things we have promised or know that we must do. Duties are a joy because we are pleasing the one we love and, for the most part, are not considered duties but rather true expressions of love for each other. Now if this be true in a human relationship, how much more is it true in relationship to our Lord Jesus? (*Love Shack*, 40-41).

Further Evidence

> *When you pray, don't babble on and on as people of other religions do. They think their prayers are answered merely by repeating their words again and again. Don't be like them, for your Father knows exactly what you need even before you ask him!* (Matthew 6:7-8)

> *Seek the Kingdom of God above all else, and live righteously, and he will give you everything you need* (Matthew 6:33).

> *Such love has no fear, because perfect love expels all fear. If we are afraid, it is for fear of punishment, and this shows that we have not fully experienced his perfect love* (1 John 4:18).

REFLECT: SEEING THE INVISIBLE

(Remember to circle, underline, or otherwise highlight any words or images that stand out to you in the devotional or the related Scriptures. Include them in your journaling response.)

Your prayers are directly related to your trust in the heart of God. You don't have to beg God to be the loving God that He is. How do you approach God—out of fear or the security of His love for you?

RESPOND

Sit with Jesus in a quiet place and read Matthew 6:7-9 as though He is speaking the words to you. Journal your reflections here.

How will I make this visible through my life today?

....

....

....

....

....

....

....

....

....

....

....

....

....

....

....

....

13

GOD'S LOVE FOR YOU IS UNDYING AND UNENDING

READ

The Father sees you in exactly the same way that He sees His firstborn Son, Jesus. His love for you is undying and His grace unending. You are not strong enough to pull yourself away from Him. Did you get that? I know this is much different from what you are used to hearing. I know it is not what you expected to read, but it is true. You are not stronger than the blood that redeemed you or the love that holds you. You should be and are intended to be certain of His love and the redeeming power of His love to hold, forgive, and restore you. You need to spend your time, energy, anointing, and creativity fulfilling His dreams for you, not trying to simply stay saved. To be faithful means to be unchanging or true. To be faithful is to stick to the deals we make.

If you have the power to keep yourself saved, then you could have saved yourself without the blood of Jesus (*Love Shack*, 52-53).

Further Evidence

For the Lord your God is living among you. He is a mighty savior. He will take delight in you with gladness. With his love, he will calm all your fears. He will rejoice over you with joyful songs (Zephaniah 3:17).

You search the Scriptures because you think they give you eternal life. But the Scriptures point to me! (John 5:39)

Just as the Father has loved Me, I have also loved you; abide in My love (John 15:9 NASB).

REFLECT: SEEING THE INVISIBLE

(Remember to circle, underline, or otherwise highlight any words or images that stand out to you in the devotional or the related Scriptures. Include them in your journaling response.)

Think of the time you have wasted trying to stay saved or earn God's love rather than simply experiencing it. Don't invest one more minute trying to perform for God what He has already performed for you in Christ.

RESPOND

As you sit quietly with Jesus, journal about the unique dream He has for you. What has God invested uniquely in you?

How will I make this visible through my life today?

14

WE ARE CLOTHED IN THE LOVE OF GOD

READ

Intimacy is the holy trust between us and our Lord that allows us to shed our fleshly selves, exposing our nakedness before Him, that He may clothe us with Himself, His unapproachable light that convinces the world that Jesus is Lord. We always thought it was our dress, our words, our preaching, or our religious demeanor that showed the world that Jesus was Lord. In fact, it is those things that make the world wonder if He really is Lord. He wants to shine through our personality, much like the brilliant sun shining through a stained glass window. The window is beautiful in itself, but with the sun shining through it, the stained glass comes alive. When we yield our lives to Him that He may shine through us, we become alive in Him. Our mere Presence convinces the world that God is alive and well on this planet. This coming together of His Person in us is true intimacy. It is a union as holy and private as the marriage bed, for it is in this union that we truly take on the divine nature, shedding the clothing of works and man-made religion (*Love Shack*, 67-68).

Further Evidence

> *Search me, O God, and know my heart; try me and know my anxious thoughts; and see if there be any hurtful way in me, and lead me in the everlasting way* (Psalm 139:23-24 NASB).

> *The glory which You have given Me I have given to them, that they may be one, just as We are one; I in them and You in Me, that they may be perfected in unity, so that the world may know that You sent Me, and loved them, even as You have loved Me* (John 17:22-23 NASB).

> *And all who have been united with Christ in baptism have put on Christ, like putting on new clothes* (Galatians 3:27).

REFLECT: SEEING THE INVISIBLE

(Remember to circle, underline, or otherwise highlight any words or images that stand out to you in the devotional or the related Scriptures. Include them in your journaling response.)

God wants to shine through your life like sun shining through a stained glass window. Yield your life to Him so that the world can see His glory through you.

RESPOND

Sit quietly with Jesus and have a conversation about His life flowing through yours.

How will I make this visible through my life today?

15

Love Brings Change As We Focus on God Rather Than Self

READ

Contrary to popular belief, it is not the intention of the Lord for us to spend our lifetime in personal introspection and analysis. Those who spend time probing the inner sanctums of their existence can easily become lost in the myriad of human complexities that we have no business dabbling in. Our minds are like unexplored caverns. We should not be spending time spelunking in caves that hide who knows what. Our focus must remain on Him and His destiny for us, with the full expectation that He will do the inner probing and changing that is required. He knows what lurks within us and He has the expertise to set us free. I suggest we serve Him and wait for Him to do the hunting. He is always on time, knowing just when to pull that old black bear out and deal with him! Times of introspection will come as you allow the Lord to show you aspects of your life that need His teaching and correction. This will undoubtedly give you a new way to live. Divine instructions are never unto death, but unto repentance and change (*Love Shack*, 79).

Further Evidence

> *Search me, O God, and know my heart; test me and know my anxious thoughts. Point out anything in me that offends you, and lead me along the path of everlasting life* (Psalm 139:23-24).

> *Therefore, since we have so great a cloud of witnesses surrounding us, let us also lay aside every encumbrance and the sin which so easily entangles us, and let us run with endurance the race that is set before us, fixing our eyes on Jesus, the author and perfecter of faith, who for the joy set before Him endured the cross, despising the shame, and has sat down at the right hand of the throne of God* (Hebrews 12:1-2 NASB).

> *Look! I stand at the door and knock. If you hear my voice and open the door, I will come in, and we will share a meal together as friends* (Revelation 3:20).

REFLECT: SEEING THE INVISIBLE

(Remember to circle, underline, or otherwise highlight any words or images that stand out to you in the devotional or the related Scriptures. Include them in your journaling response.)

As you cultivate the reality of God's Presence, your focus shifts to God. Our focus on God changes us. Behold and reflect now the face of Jesus as you see Him and allow Him to assure you of His love for you.

RESPOND

Journal your experience here as you focus on the Presence of Jesus.

How will I make this visible through my life today?

....

....

....

....

....

....

....

....

....

....

....

....

....

16

LOVE BRINGS WHOLENESS OUT OF BROKENNESS

READ

Wholeness emerges from brokenness. Wholeness, when God is making you whole, is a completion of soul and spirit that can only be accomplished by the Cross. For many, brokenness is where the process ends. Its pain is too difficult and its process too unbearable. *Brokenness* is a word that I have feared for many years. I did my best to avoid it. But, and I say this cautiously, I am glad brokenness caught up to me. In fact, it did not catch up with me; it ran me over as I went recklessly into the realms of spirit that I knew little about and was completely unprepared to understand and deal with. I had spent my life mimicking those I admired and found myself powerless and empty. Avoiding the process of brokenness is not the recommended way of maturity. Through brokenness, we are retooled by the Spirit of the Lord so the Presence of Jesus can shine brightly with all His love, mercy, and compassion. The more we yield to Him, the more we shine with Him. The more we accept our weakness, the stronger we become in Him (*Love Shack*, 92-93).

Further Evidence

Come, let us return to the Lord. He has torn us to pieces; now he will heal us. He has injured us; now he will bandage our wounds (Hosea 6:1).

And He has said to me, "My grace is sufficient for you, for power is perfected in weakness." Most gladly, therefore, I will rather boast about my weaknesses, so that the power of Christ may dwell in me. Therefore I am well content with weaknesses, with insults, with distresses, with persecutions, with difficulties, for Christ's sake; for when I am weak, then I am strong (2 Corinthians 12:9-10 NASB).

REFLECT: SEEING THE INVISIBLE

(Remember to circle, underline, or otherwise highlight any words or images that stand out to you in the devotional or the related Scriptures. Include them in your journaling response.)

The brokenness in your life allows you to experience wholeness. God sometimes takes us apart to put us back together again.

RESPOND

In the Presence of Jesus, wrapped in His love, reflect on how God is stepping into your weaknesses with His strength. Journal your thoughts here.

How will I make this visible through my life today?

17

TRUE LOVE LIVES FOREVER

READ

True love never ends and can never be destroyed. True love cannot be reasoned with, nor can it be reasoned away, for it has little to do with the intellect but it has everything to do with that which the intellect can never touch. True love dwells so much higher than understanding, in a dimension where love rules and the mind serves true love. Love will always, always, find a way. Love always prevails. Love always gathers. Love always forgives. Love always heals. Love understands. Love feeds the world with compassion and mercy. True love yields to the forgiving nature of her Lord and accurately represents His grace in every respect. Love lives forever *(Romancing the Divine,* 9).

Further Evidence

> *Such love has no fear, because perfect love expels all fear. If we are afraid, it is for fear of punishment, and this shows that we have not fully experienced his perfect love* (1 John 4:18).

Your unfailing love is better than life itself; how I praise you! (Psalm 63:3)

The faithful love of the Lord never ends! His mercies never cease. Great is his faithfulness; his mercies begin afresh each morning (Lamentations 3:22-23).

REFLECT: SEEING THE INVISIBLE

(Remember to circle, underline, or otherwise highlight any words or images that stand out to you in the devotional or the related Scriptures. Include them in your journaling response.)

God's true love for you does not depend upon your understanding of it; only that you receive it. Dare to receive it now.

RESPOND

Gather yourself into the personal Presence of Jesus and exchange your fears for His perfect love. Journal your reflections here.

How will I make this visible through my life today?

18

True Love Seems Crazy to Those Who Have Not Experienced It

Read

Predictably, true love will always have its detractors. "Are you crazy?" is the inevitable question from these who have either never experienced true love or who have forgotten its illogical and all-consuming captivity. And just like everyone else who has ever been moonstruck by this...this unexplainable, undeniable supernatural force, you respond with a wistful, far-away look in your eyes, "Yes. If by finding true love you mean crazy, then, yes, I believe I am."

"But don't you realize what this means?" the grilling continues. "Don't you understand what an uproar this will cause? People will think you have gone off the deep end for sure. They will say you have gone into heresy. People will write about you in their books!"

"If true love is heresy, then I am happy to be in heresy," you respond with unmistakable resolve in your voice. "True love is worth the ridicule of man. If I am to be accused of anything so heinous, let it be for this love. May the accusation be that I fell in love, and that love consumed me, and drove me to pay any price for it" (*Romancing the Divine*, 8).

Further Evidence

> *Place me like a seal over your heart, like a seal on your arm. For love is as strong as death, its jealousy as enduring as the grave. Love flashes like fire, the brightest kind of flame* (Song of Solomon 8:6).

> *If it seems we are crazy, it is to bring glory to God. And if we are in our right minds, it is for your benefit* (2 Corinthians 5:13).

> *Most important of all, continue to show deep love for each other, for love covers a multitude of sins* (1 Peter 4:8).

REFLECT: SEEING THE INVISIBLE

(Remember to circle, underline, or otherwise highlight any words or images that stand out to you in the devotional or the related Scriptures. Include them in your journaling response.)

The love of God makes little sense to the world. Beloved, stop trying to make sense of God's love and just be loved! Sit quietly with Jesus and allow yourself to believe that you are loved by God.

RESPOND

Write down any obstacles you believe might prevent you from receiving the love of God. Now ask Jesus how He has overcome those obstacles.

How will I make this visible through my life today?

....

....

....

....

....

....

....

....

....

....

....

....

....

....

....

....

....

TRUE LOVE IS MORE THAN RELIGION

READ

True love will never sing the songs of a hollow religion and is not pacified with pointless ritual. Love cannot coexist with legalism and does not interact well with hypocrisy. If she is banished, it is a good thing, for it will allow more time to be with the Lord. If she is condemned, she will smile quietly, respectably, of course. Condemnation is the last course of a clueless man. Love cannot be condemned. Love feeds the world with compassion and mercy. True love yields to the forgiving nature of her Lord and accurately represents His grace in every respect.

But let me encourage you to step out of the restraints of religious control. Let your spirit go. Give in to the yearning within, and come, let us romance the Divine together. Who knows? We may find true love (*Romancing the Divine*, 9-10).

Further Evidence

So you have not received a spirit that makes you fearful slaves. Instead, you received God's Spirit when he adopted you as his own children. Now we call him, "Abba, Father" (Romans 8:15).

Love is patient and kind. Love is not jealous or boastful or proud or rude. It does not demand its own way. It is not irritable, and it keeps no record of being wronged. It does not rejoice about injustice but rejoices whenever the truth wins out. Love never gives up, never loses faith, is always hopeful, and endures through every circumstance (1 Corinthians 13:4-7).

For God hath not given us the spirit of fear; but of power, and of love, and of a sound mind (2 Timothy 1:7 KJV).

REFLECT: SEEING THE INVISIBLE

(Remember to circle, underline, or otherwise highlight any words or images that stand out to you in the devotional or the related Scriptures. Include them in your journaling response.)

Love is a true representation of God that makes God real to the world. You can live out the purity of that love. Now, as you sit in the Presence of God, speak His favorite name for Himself several times—Abba, Abba, Abba.

RESPOND

Write down what your heart feels as you call out His name—Abba.

How will I make this visible through my life today?

20

I Am Loved!

Read

He loves me—little ole me. He wants me. It does not matter what the religious right or the religious left may say. I am loved and there is nothing that can separate me from that love. Now that I have found Him whom my soul doth love, I will not run *to* Him; I will run *with* Him. I will not work *for* Him; I will work *with* Him. I will not worship to *get* His attention. I will worship because I *have* His all. I won't worship to *gain* His favor but because I *have* His favor. I know I am in the palm of His hand. I know He has my life under His control. Therein does my search forever change. Therein does my heart rejoice and my spirit rest. I please Him. I just please Him. I know it sounds awfully strange, but I can get used to it. I please the Lord. I bring a smile to His face and a song to His heart. He wants to be with me. He wants to live within me (*Romancing the Divine,* 188).

Further Evidence

> *But whatever I am now, it is all because God poured out his special favor on me—and not without results. For I have worked harder than any of the other apostles; yet it was not I but God who was working through me by his grace* (1 Corinthians 15:10).

> *This is a trustworthy saying, and everyone should accept it: "Christ Jesus came into the world to save sinners"—and I am the worst of them all. But God had mercy on me so that Christ Jesus could use me as a prime example of his great patience with even the worst sinners. Then others will realize that they, too, can believe in him and receive eternal life. All honor and glory to God forever and ever! He is the eternal King, the unseen one who never dies; he alone is God. Amen* (1 Timothy 1:15-17).

REFLECT: SEEING THE INVISIBLE

(Remember to circle, underline, or otherwise highlight any words or images that stand out to you in the devotional or the related Scriptures. Include them in your journaling response.)

You please the Lord because of His great love for you, not because of what you can do for Him. Stop searching for what isn't lost and stop trying to earn what is already yours freely in Christ.

RESPOND

Take a few minutes in the Presence of Jesus and allow Him to pour the precious oil of His grace over you. Write your response to His love here.

How will I make this visible through my life today?

....

....

....

....

....

....

....

....

....

....

....

....

....

....

....

....

....

....

....

21

LOVE CHANGES THE WORLD THROUGH US

READ

You are loved beyond measure. Whether you ever do anything for God's glory or not, you will be forever unconditionally loved. Your worth is never to be measured by what you do or accomplish. Never is your value based on works. You are worth everything to God just because you *are*. You are His treasure and His delight. Your entrance into the world was a significant, blessed event for Him. Your life *is* significant! You don't *have* to make a mark for His glory in the earth—but you *get* to! Mankind was blessed in the very beginning by God when He said, *"Be fruitful and multiply; fill the earth and subdue it; have dominion over the fish of the sea, over the birds of the air, and over every living thing that moves on the earth"* (Gen. 1:28 NKJV). You do not have to be fruitful and fill the earth in order to be loved, but you will be frustrated if you don't because you were created for this purpose (*Change the World*, 30).

Further Evidence

> The Spirit of the Lord is upon me, for he has anointed me to bring Good News to the poor. He has sent me to proclaim that captives will be released, that the blind will see, that the oppressed will be set free, and that the time of the Lord's favor has come (Luke 4:18-19).

> But we who live by the Spirit eagerly wait to receive by faith the righteousness God has promised to us. For when we place our faith in Christ Jesus, there is no benefit in being circumcised or being uncircumcised. What is important is faith expressing itself in love (Galatians 5:5-6).

REFLECT: SEEING THE INVISIBLE

(Remember to circle, underline, or otherwise highlight any words or images that stand out to you in the devotional or the related Scriptures. Include them in your journaling response.)

You are loved because you *are*, not because of what you do or give. Now allow the love of God to influence the world through your life!

RESPOND

In the Presence of Jesus, think of another person or people group who need the love of God and pray for them.

How will I make this visible through my life today?

Love Changes the World Through Us

22

OUR IDENTITY IS BASED ON LOVE NOT LABOR

READ

When we base our identity in our own efforts to be acceptable to a seemingly distant God, we will easily judge someone else's value based on how they live their lives in relation to the rules of behavior we are struggling with ourselves. In that reality, there is no family of God, only the business of religion. Holiness gets defined by my separateness, not from sin but apart from everything and everyone not acceptable to my fear. Real holiness is a life stewarding my intimacy with the Father and living out that love in relation to others. Grace is living with a God-consciousness, not a sin-consciousness. This is the Kingdom to which Jesus was inviting people. This is the quantum leap. Our identity is shaped by the reality we choose to live in. The depths of love, joy, peace, and every other fruit of His Spirit we experience is determined by that reality (*Change the World*, 52).

Further Evidence

But whatever I am now, it is all because God poured out his special favor on me—and not without results. For I have worked harder than any of the other apostles; yet it was not I but God who was working through me by his grace (1 Corinthians 15:10).

Imitate God, therefore, in everything you do, because you are his dear children (Ephesians 5:1).

Dear friends, let us continue to love one another, for love comes from God. Anyone who loves is a child of God and knows God (1 John 4:7).

REFLECT: SEEING THE INVISIBLE

(Remember to circle, underline, or otherwise highlight any words or images that stand out to you in the devotional or the related Scriptures. Include them in your journaling response.)

By the grace of God through Christ you have a new identity that can affect the world around you. That new identity serves as the connection between Heaven and earth.

RESPOND

Sit in the Presence of Jesus and write down the truths of your new identity in Jesus that stand out to you.

How will I make this visible through my life today?

23

JESUS IS THE PATTERN LOVER

READ

There is no greater pattern for a modern believer than to see Him [Jesus Christ] as the *Pattern Lover*. He loves when others hate. He reaches out His hands to those who close theirs to Him. His love for humanity does not give room to return anything else but what is in Him, no matter what comes to Him from those who reject Him. There is nothing within Him that can be stirred up against those who hate Him because there is nothing but love within Him. There is no doubt that the overriding force in the life of Jesus is His compelling love, His focused compassion toward humanity (*I Am a Son*, 152-153).

Further Evidence

Yahweh! The Lord! The God of compassion and mercy! I am slow to anger and filled with unfailing love and faithfulness (Exodus 34:6).

And walk in love, as Christ also has loved us and given Himself for us, an offering and a sacrifice to God for a sweet-smelling aroma (Ephesians 5:2 NKJV).

Such love has no fear, because perfect love expels all fear. If we are afraid, it is for fear of punishment, and this shows that we have not fully experienced his perfect love (1 John 4:18).

We love Him because He first loved us (1 John 4:19 NKJV).

REFLECT: SEEING THE INVISIBLE

(Remember to circle, underline, or otherwise highlight any words or images that stand out to you in the devotional or the related Scriptures. Include them in your journaling response.)

Your life holds some kind of pattern, whether one of compassion or self-focus. Jesus came to give you the opportunity to change the pattern of your life to one of loving God, other people, and yourself. Who is your life about?

RESPOND

Take time to examine the pattern of your life now in the Presence of Jesus. Write down what you see.

How will I make this visible through my life today?

....

....

....

24

CHILDREN OF GOD, NOT HIRED SERVANTS

READ

Do you see with the eyes of a servant? Being a servant is a powerful part of our life in God, but Jesus invited the disciples to much more. A servant may only see that field in terms of the task. People are simply "the harvest," a goal. A servant's relationship to his master is in the form of orders, not intimacy. If the servant fails, he lives in shame, because there is nowhere else to go. Servants have little relationship with each other and even less freedom. The upgraded reality of "friend" brings a new perspective. Friends have far greater relationship and know they are chosen, not hired or indentured. But God doesn't stop there. He invites us to know Him as sons and daughters, as unconditionally loved children. Sons aren't afraid of losing relationship with the King; they are always sons. When they hear a call for battle, they don't see it as a draft in which they have no choice; they see it as expanding the Kingdom of which they are royal inheritors and co-laborers. They see the fields as dearly loved brothers and sisters who are that inheritance, their family in joy and love forever (*Change the World*, 52).

Further Evidence

> *See how very much our Father loves us, for he calls us his children, and that is what we are! But the people who belong to this world don't recognize that we are God's children because they don't know him* (1 John 3:1).

> *But to all who believed him and accepted him, he gave the right to become children of God. They are reborn— not with a physical birth resulting from human passion or plan, but a birth that comes from God* (John 1:12-13).

> *So you have not received a spirit that makes you fearful slaves. Instead, you received God's Spirit when he adopted you as his own children. Now we call him, "Abba, Father"* (Romans 8:15).

REFLECT: SEEING THE INVISIBLE

(Remember to circle, underline, or otherwise highlight any words or images that stand out to you in the devotional or the related Scriptures. Include them in your journaling response.)

How do you see yourself—as a hireling of God or beloved child? Praise God that He makes us His children and heirs to His Kingdom.

RESPOND

Take time to think and write about how God has called you into His business.

How will I make this visible through my life today?

....

....

....

....

....

....

....

....

....

....

....

....

....

....

....

....

25

WE ARE HELD SECURELY IN THE PASSIONATE LOVE OF GOD

READ

There is a depth of relationship in fellowship with Him that only those who have a burning passion for Him will ever experience. He wants us to *run* after Him. He does not want us to be content or satisfied with what we have or what we've experienced. There is a place of shelter, a relationship, a reality of the spiritual Presence of God that is for our experience in this life that will only be attained as we yield to Him with all our heart, with all our soul, with all our mind, and with all our strength. We too easily forget there is a vastness and limitlessness that God has for us. It is His manifest Presence, and it is there for all who will respond—and keep on responding—to God's call in their lives (*Manifest Presence*, 120).

Further Evidence

> *And you must love the Lord your God with all your heart, all your soul, and all your strength* (Deuteronomy 6:5).

And now, Israel, what does the Lord your God require of you? He requires only that you fear the Lord your God, and live in a way that pleases him, and love him and serve him with all your heart and soul (Deuteronomy 10:12).

How precious is your unfailing love, O God! All humanity finds shelter in the shadow of your wings (Psalm 36:7).

Let all that I am praise the Lord; with my whole heart, I will praise his holy name (Psalm 103:1).

REFLECT: SEEING THE INVISIBLE

(Remember to circle, underline, or otherwise highlight any words or images that stand out to you in the devotional or the related Scriptures. Include them in your journaling response.)

Have you reached a place of contentment in your relationship with God? How are you pursuing Him daily? Take a few minutes to think about your pursuit of God—not what He does for you, but who He *is* to you.

RESPOND

Sit in the Presence of Jesus and journal your reflections here. How will I make this visible through my life today?

26

GOD IN CHRIST BRINGS US TO LOVE AS HE LOVES

READ

True union [with God in Christ] is not ultimately an inward journey. Instead, it causes you to look outward. Union helps you to understand your oneness with the Lord. When this union is cultivated, you will see as He sees, love as He loves, and gather as He gathers. How does this happen? It happens when your understanding of the process is changed. You know that He is taking care of your needs, desires, and pain. As a result, your focus no longer needs to be upon yourself. The Presence then flows from you to the world. You become driven in the same way He is driven—by His love, to meet the needs of those around you (*The Voice*, 20).

Further Evidence

> *Look at the lilies and how they grow. They don't work or make their clothing, yet Solomon in all his glory was not dressed as beautifully as they are* (Luke 12:27).

Dear friends, I am not writing a new commandment for you; rather it is an old one you have had from the very beginning. This old commandment—to love one another—is the same message you heard before (1 John 2:7).

By his divine power, God has given us everything we need for living a godly life. We have received all of this by coming to know him, the one who called us to himself by means of his marvelous glory and excellence (2 Peter 1:3).

REFLECT: SEEING THE INVISIBLE

(Remember to circle, underline, or otherwise highlight any words or images that stand out to you in the devotional or the related Scriptures. Include them in your journaling response.)

Love is not just a concept; it must be lived to be seen. How does the love of God flow through your life to other people?

RESPOND

Sit quietly with Jesus and ask Him to remind you of the people around you who need love.

How will I make this visible through my life today?

....

....

....

....

27

GOD SENT HIS ONLY SON TO RESCUE US FROM OURSELVES

READ

Hah! Here is the irony. I thought I was trying to get His [God's] attention all this time. I thought this burning desire for meaning and relevance within my heart was just there, almost by accident. But He wanted me so much that He put that burning desire for Him within me. So I would search out His love and His Presence. He has romanced me, indeed! It is, without question, the ultimate romance. For God so loved the world, me individually, me personally, that He planted desire in my heart, that I may be overwhelmed with that desire to run after Him with everything that is within me (*Romancing the Divine*, 187).

Further Evidence

> *Great is the Lord! He is most worthy of praise! No one can measure his greatness* (Psalm 145:3).

For this is how God loved the world: He gave his one and only Son, so that everyone who believes in him will not perish but have eternal life (John 3:16).

For he has rescued us from the kingdom of darkness and transferred us into the Kingdom of his dear Son (Colossians 1:13).

We love each other because he loved us first (1 John 4:19).

REFLECT: SEEING THE INVISIBLE

(Remember to circle, underline, or otherwise highlight any words or images that stand out to you in the devotional or the related Scriptures. Include them in your journaling response.)

God is drawing you into the possibility of a deep and intimate pursuit—your pursuit of God and God's pursuit of you! Take time to consider God's pursuit of you.

RESPOND

Journal about the history of God's pursuit of you and how you came to pursue Him back.

How will I make this visible through my life today?

....

....

....

....

....

28

As We Yield to Jesus His Power Works Through Us

READ

It is true that when we see Him as He is, we become like Him. The more we see Him, the more His passion begins to rule our heart. His love begins to flood our soul. We begin to respond to the Holy Spirit as Jesus responded when He walked the earth. There is little significance in me as a mere man, but there is full assurance, full completion of His love in Him. We often believe we can go it in our strength from Him. It is as though we believe the natural gifts God gives us are almost enough to fulfill our destiny. But the personal talents and gifts God gives us blossom exponentially when we yield everything we have and everything we are to Jesus. For we who believe are more than mere humans. We are human vessels filled with God. So we are becoming all God-filled believers just as Jesus was (*God Watchers*, 40).

Further Evidence

> *Put on your new nature, and be renewed as you learn to know your Creator and become like him* (Colossians 3:10).

For it was the Father's good pleasure for all the fullness to dwell in Him (Colossians 1:19 NASB).

And so, dear brothers and sisters, I plead with you to give your bodies to God because of all he has done for you. Let them be a living and holy sacrifice—the kind he will find acceptable. This is truly the way to worship him. Don't copy the behavior and customs of this world, but let God transform you into a new person by changing the way you think. Then you will learn to know God's will for you, which is good and pleasing and perfect (Romans 12:1-2).

REFLECT: SEEING THE INVISIBLE

(Remember to circle, underline, or otherwise highlight any words or images that stand out to you in the devotional or the related Scriptures. Include them in your journaling response.)

Spiritual gifts disconnected from the Giver are not enough to fulfill your destiny in God. God gave you gifts for His eternal purpose.

RESPOND

Sit quietly acknowledging the Presence of Jesus and consider how you establish His Kingdom in your own unique ways. Journal your reflections here.

How will I make this visible through my life today?

29

LOOK AT JESUS!

READ

The more I see Him, the more I become like Him. Seeing Him as He truly is ignites a supernatural transformation that education alone cannot hope to accomplish. Seeing Him changes our spiritual DNA from self-centeredness to Christ-centeredness. This transformation is a continuous process of becoming a new person in Christ, of putting on His mind, living by His faith, and doing the works of His Father and mine. I begin to see as He sees, hear as He hears, and love as He loves. My motivation is no longer self-promotion. I am not looking for a "word" to impress anyone, nor do I write my own marketing plan as though I have a comedy routine or set of songs to sing and peddle from town to town. As I see, I do. If I do not see, I do nothing. I am becoming like Him—single-minded in love, restoration, and wholeness (*God Watchers*, 127).

Further Evidence

For, "Who can know the Lord's thoughts? Who knows enough to teach him?" But we understand these things, for we have the mind of Christ (1 Corinthians 2:16).

So all of us who have had that veil removed can see and reflect the glory of the Lord. And the Lord—who is the Spirit—makes us more and more like him as we are changed into his glorious image (2 Corinthians 3:18).

And all who have been united with Christ in baptism have put on Christ, like putting on new clothes (Galatians 3:27).

REFLECT: SEEING THE INVISIBLE

(Remember to circle, underline, or otherwise highlight any words or images that stand out to you in the devotional or the related Scriptures. Include them in your journaling response.)

Do you ever ask yourself why you do what you do? This is especially true in your Kingdom life.

Reflect on your motivations for relationship with Him and through Jesus to the people around you.

RESPOND

Sit quietly with Jesus and journal your reflections here. How will I make this visible though my life today?

....

....

Look at Jesus!

30

CONFIDENCE IN GOD'S LOVE IS ALL THAT MATTERS

READ

I am with Him on the Mercy Seat where mercy and grace run freely and forgiveness strengthens me to go on. The stench of sin wants me to carry guilt and live in depression, but I have experienced His love. I will not go back to guilt. I will not go back to shame. To be sure, each failure is a humbling experience. I realize how weak I am. I get frustrated, and I wonder how He can endure my weakness another minute, especially when it seems as though I fail again and again (*Romancing the Divine*, 182).

FURTHER EVIDENCE

The eternal God is your refuge, and his everlasting arms are under you (Deuteronomy 33:27).

Can anything ever separate us from Christ's love? Does it mean he no longer loves us if we have trouble or calamity, or are persecuted, or hungry, or destitute, or in danger, or threatened with death? (As the Scriptures say, "For your sake we are killed every day; we are being slaughtered like sheep.") No, despite all these things, overwhelming victory is ours through Christ, who loved us (Romans 8:35-37).

Then He said to me, "It is done. I am the Alpha and the Omega, the beginning and the end. I will give to the one who thirsts from the spring of the water of life without cost. He who overcomes will inherit these things, and I will be his God and he will be My son" (Revelation 21:6-7 NASB).

REFLECT: SEEING THE INVISIBLE

(Remember to circle, underline, or otherwise highlight any words or images that stand out to you in the devotional or the related Scriptures. Include them in your journaling response.)

You are safe in the embrace of God's love for you. The love of God cannot merely be a pleasant thought; it must become a personal reality. Nothing can come between God's face and yours unless you allow it.

RESPOND

Sit quietly with Jesus and consider what might keep you from believing the love of God for you personally. Journal your reflections here.

How will I make this visible though my life today?

LIVING IN THE PRESENCE OF GOD

31

God Wants to Live with Us, to Make Himself Real to Us

Read

There are basically two ways to look at the Presence of God. There is first of all His omniPresence—God is everywhere. We know that God is everywhere, whether we can sense Him or not. God fills the earth. Wherever you go, God will hear your prayer, because His omniPresence covers the earth. But there is a more specific type of His Presence—His manifest Presence. God's manifest Presence is revealed whenever He makes Himself real to *you*, personally. This takes place when He makes Himself real to you *in your spirit* and you know beyond a shadow of a doubt that God has spoken to your heart. You know He has manifested Himself to you; you are experiencing His manifest Presence (*Manifest Presence*, 20-21).

Further Evidence

> *Then I will live among the people of Israel and be their God, and they will know that I am the Lord their God.*

I am the one who brought them out of the land of Egypt so that I could live among them. I am the Lord their God (Exodus 29:45-46).

I heard a loud shout from the throne, saying, "Look, God's home is now among his people! He will live with them, and they will be his people. God himself will be with them" (Revelation 21:3).

For we are the temple of the living God. As God said: "I will live in them and walk among them. I will be their God, and they will be my people (2 Corinthians 6:16).

REFLECT: SEEING THE INVISIBLE

(Remember to circle, underline, or otherwise highlight any words or images that stand out to you in the devotional or the related Scriptures. Include them in your journaling response.)

God's Presence is more than a theoretical possibility; it is a reality manifested through your very life. God becomes visible to the world as you focus every aspect of your life on Him. Reflect on the ways God is becoming more a focus in your life and perhaps where you might invite Him to do so.

RESPOND

As you sit quietly with Jesus journal your reflections here. How will I make this visible through my life today?

....

....

32

GOD BECOMES MORE REAL TO US AS WE WALK WITH HIM

READ

We walk by faith, not by sight (see 2 Cor. 5:7), but it is not *for* our faith that God chooses to reveal Himself to us. It is rather in *response* to our faith that God manifests Himself. Our faith moves Him to transcend time and space and respond *in* the natural realm to our faith. God has always delighted in manifesting Himself in a physical, tangible way to His people. His purpose from the very beginning has been to be a manifest God to His people. The entire purpose of redemption was to cleanse for Himself a people to whom He could reveal Himself and with whom He could live in a manifested way. God delights in flowing with and moving with His people. The dictionary defines *manifest* as: "readily perceived by the senses; easily understood or recognized by the mind; obvious." This is how God wants to make Himself known to us in these last days (*Manifest Presence*, 22).

Further Evidence

> *The Lord went ahead of them. He guided them during the day with a pillar of cloud, and he provided light at night with a pillar of fire. This allowed them to travel by day or by night. And the Lord did not remove the pillar of cloud or pillar of fire from its place in front of the people* (Exodus 13:21-22).

> *For we live by believing and not by seeing* (2 Corinthians 5:7).

> *Christ is the visible image of the invisible God. He existed before anything was created and is supreme over all creation* (Colossians 1:15).

REFLECT: SEEING THE INVISIBLE

(Remember to circle, underline, or otherwise highlight any words or images that stand out to you in the devotional or the related Scriptures. Include them in your journaling response.)

God revealed Himself through Jesus Christ. The world now sees Christ through you as you live close to Him. How is your life reflecting the Presence of God?

RESPOND

Write your response here in the Presence of Jesus who loves you so much.

How will this become visible through my life today?

33

TRANSFORMED INTO
ANOINTED WARRIORS

READ

On the Day of Pentecost, God's Presence was manifested with cloven tongues of fire and a rushing, mighty wind sweeping through the place in which the disciples were gathered. God's Presence was so evident that they were able to get in touch with Him through their five senses. What exhilaration and what power energized them from within as they experienced the manifest Presence of God! (See Acts 2:1-4; 14-38.) Their confidence and assurance in His Presence gave them the ability to preach with great boldness as the Holy Spirit moved upon them with power. We find Peter and John and the rest of the disciples praying to the Lord for strength and ability in Acts 4:31: *"And when they had prayed, the place where they had gathered together was shaken, and they were all filled with the Holy Spirit and began to speak the word of God with boldness"* (NASB). His manifest Presence transforms mere mortal men, cowering before fleshly strongholds and threats, into mighty men of anointing and power (*Manifest Presence*, 25).

Further Evidence

> *On the day of Pentecost all the believers were meeting together in one place. Suddenly, there was a sound from heaven like the roaring of a mighty windstorm, and it filled the house where they were sitting. Then, what looked like flames or tongues of fire appeared and settled on each of them. And everyone present was filled with the Holy Spirit and began speaking in other languages, as the Holy Spirit gave them this ability* (Acts 2:1-4).

> *And so, dear brothers and sisters, I plead with you to give your bodies to God because of all he has done for you. Let them be a living and holy sacrifice—the kind he will find acceptable. This is truly the way to worship him. Don't copy the behavior and customs of this world, but let God transform you into a new person by changing the way you think. Then you will learn to know God's will for you, which is good and pleasing and perfect* (Romans 12:1-2).

REFLECT: SEEING THE INVISIBLE

(Remember to circle, underline, or otherwise highlight any words or images that stand out to you in the devotional or the related Scriptures. Include them in your journaling response.)

On the day of Pentecost people were empowered by the Spirit of God to bring the realities of Heaven to earth. Ask the Father to immerse you now in the Spirit.

RESPOND

Journal your thoughts and experiences here, immersed in the Holy Spirit.

How will this become visible through my life today?

34

DIFFICULTIES AND CHALLENGES INVITE US TO DEEPER AWARENESS OF THE PRESENCE OF GOD

READ

In our day, we are beginning to see a continual fulfilling of Emmanuel—God with us. God has always desired to live and dwell and manifest Himself in the midst of His people. As He walked with Adam in the cool of the evening (see Gen. 3:8), God also wants to walk with us so that we will become a people who will experience His Presence, His power, and His glory in a tangible way. The days directly ahead of us will require this. Periods of tribulation and hardship have always driven the people of God into His Presence, thus experiencing His power in mighty ways. Difficult times press God's people into Him so that they, too, will experience His manifest Presence (*Manifest Presence*, 27).

Further Evidence

Enoch lived 365 years, walking in close fellowship with God. Then one day he disappeared, because God took him (Genesis 5:23-24).

O Jerusalem, Jerusalem, the city that kills the prophets and stones God's messengers! How often I have wanted to gather your children together as a hen protects her chicks beneath her wings, but you wouldn't let me (Luke 13:34).

So I say, let the Holy Spirit guide your lives. Then you won't be doing what your sinful nature craves. ...But the Holy Spirit produces this kind of fruit in our lives: love, joy, peace, patience, kindness, goodness, faithfulness, gentleness, and self-control. There is no law against these things! (Galatians 5:16,22-23)

REFLECT: SEEING THE INVISIBLE

(Remember to circle, underline, or otherwise highlight any words or images that stand out to you in the devotional or the related Scriptures. Include them in your journaling response.)

Adam walked with God in the Spirit. Enoch walked so closely with God that he disappeared into Him. You may walk in the Spirit with God so that your life merges into His.

RESPOND

Journal here about where you most sense the Presence of God and where you might be more aware of Him.

How will this become visible through my life today?

35

GOD WANTS TO LIVE IN AND THROUGH US

READ

God has always sought a people in whom He could *abide.* We have heard of the visitations of God, but it has never been His intention simply to *visit* His people. He has always looked for a place of *abiding,* where His Presence could dwell permanently. God wants to come into our hearts to dwell perpetually, to rule and reign through us. He does not come simply to save us, not simply to fill us with His Spirit, but that His Lordship might be manifested, both in us and in all of those around us. Our only hope is for the glory of God to descend upon us and dwell within us. Only then can God have His way in our lives. Only then will we be changed into what God wants us to be. Our hope, our only hope, is for the glory of God to be made manifest (*Manifest Presence,* 32).

Further Evidence

Who may worship in your sanctuary, Lord? Who may enter your presence on your holy hill? Those who lead blameless lives and do what is right, speaking the truth from sincere hearts (Psalm 15:1-2).

Jesus replied, "All who love me will do what I say. My Father will love them, and we will come and make our home with each of them" (John 14:23).

So all of us who have had that veil removed can see and reflect the glory of the Lord. And the Lord—who is the Spirit—makes us more and more like him as we are changed into his glorious image (2 Corinthians 3:18).

REFLECT: SEEING THE INVISIBLE

(Remember to circle, underline, or otherwise highlight any words or images that stand out to you in the devotional or the related Scriptures. Include them in your journaling response.)

God does not want to come to your house for a visit or a cup of coffee; He wants to move in and live with and through you. Make room for God. Welcome and give Him the most comfortable chair in the house!

RESPOND

As you sit quietly with Jesus, reflect on those areas of your life He wants to move in. Journal your thoughts and reflections here.

How will I make this visible through my life today?

....

....

36

God Wants to Share the Intimate Secrets of His Heart with Us

Read

We serve a God who wants to communicate with His people. We serve a God who wants to be intimate with His people. He doesn't want to pull surprises on us. He wants us to know what He's up to. Jesus said, *"I am no longer calling you 'slaves,' because a slave doesn't know what his master is doing. I am calling you 'friends,' because I have revealed to you everything which I have heard from my father"* (John 15:15). The Lord is calling us to a place of intimacy where He can speak to us and share His innermost desires with us. God wants to tell us His secrets. The many-faceted wisdom of God that has been hidden for ages and ages contains the very secrets He wants to speak to our hearts. That which is hidden to the rest of creation God wants to manifest to us. Such is the desire in the heart of God to have intimate friendship and fellowship with us (*Manifest Presence*, 38).

Further Evidence

> *Jesus said, "I am no longer calling you 'slaves,' because a slave doesn't know what his master is doing. I am calling you 'friends,' because I have revealed to you everything which I have heard from my father"* (John 15:15).

> *For all who are led by the Spirit of God are children of God. So you have not received a spirit that makes you fearful slaves. Instead, you received God's Spirit when he adopted you as his own children. Now we call him, "Abba, Father"* (Romans 8:14-15).

> *And because we are his children, God has sent the Spirit of his Son into our hearts, prompting us to call out, "Abba, Father"* (Galatians 4:6).

REFLECT: SEEING THE INVISIBLE

(Remember to circle, underline, or otherwise highlight any words or images that stand out to you in the devotional or the related Scriptures. Include them in your journaling response.)

God through Christ has brought you into the family business. Do business! Take time in the Presence of Jesus to allow Him to invite you to join Him in what He is doing around you, in your family, your neighborhood, your job, etc.

RESPOND

Journal what you sense Jesus inviting you into here. How will I make this visible though my life today?

37

GOD'S KINGDOM WANTS TO MOVE IN WITH US

READ

God is getting ready "to upset the apple cart." He will cause so many things to happen that simply don't fit with our preconceived ideas. But God is on the move and I believe He will establish His Presence within us. The Presence of God will become so manifest in the midst of His people that healing and restoration will come as someone brings forth a word, or in a time of worship, or just as people pray for one another. To a degree, this is already happening, but there will soon be a great acceleration of this kind of activity. There will be a sense of His Presence that is so real that we won't have to convince one another that God is here. God will manifest Himself in the midst of the assembly. His manifest Presence may not take the form of a literal fire by night or a literal smoke by day, but it will be a reality nonetheless. The children of Israel could look at the manifest Presence of God and say, "There is God," and so will we be able to do. God will so move in the midst of His people that we will be able to say, "God is moving, and there He is" (*Manifest Presence*, 38).

Further Evidence

I heard a loud shout from the throne, saying, "Look, God's home is now among his people! He will live with them, and they will be his people. God himself will be with them" (Revelations 21:3).

"But this is the new covenant I will make with the people of Israel on that day," says the Lord. "I will put my instructions deep within them, and I will write them on their hearts. I will be their God, and they will be my people" (Jeremiah 31:33).

Jesus replied, "The Kingdom of God can't be detected by visible signs. You won't be able to say, 'Here it is!' or 'It's over there!' For the Kingdom of God is already among you" (Luke 17:20-21).

REFLECT: SEEING THE INVISIBLE

(Remember to circle, underline, or otherwise highlight any words or images that stand out to you in the devotional or the related Scriptures. Include them in your journaling response.)

You might think you know what God is up to around you. Now allow God to upset your theological applecart. What has God done around you that was unexpected in the past?

RESPOND

Journal here about where you desire to see the reality of God's Presence in your life today.

How will I make this visible through my life today?

38

THE PRESENCE OF THE LORD IS OUR PROTECTION

READ

Whether it be in the form of a dove or in fire, God wants to establish Himself in us so that His Presence will be manifested. It can be in the church, and it can also be in our homes and in our jobs. When it happens, people will look at you and see Jesus—not because you preach to them, but because your life radiates His manifest Presence. God is manifesting Himself to us. This manifest Presence is what will bring the nations to the Church. It is His manifest Presence that protects us. It's His manifest Presence that gives us the peace of mind and peace of heart to know that *"At your side 1,000 people may die, or even 10,000 right beside you. But you will not be hurt"* (Ps. 91:7 ICB). This, then, is my peace, and this, then, is my rest. It does not come from some mental assent of God's being everywhere, of His Presence being everywhere, nor is it just intellectually agreeing with that statement. It is emotionally, personally, and spiritually experiencing His Presence in the kind of reality that says, "I know that I know that I know that Jesus Christ is with me" (*Manifest Presence*, 50).

Further Evidence

> *What shall we say about such wonderful things as these? If God is for us, who can ever be against us?* (Romans 8:31)

> *I trust in God, so why should I be afraid? What can mere mortals do to me?* (Psalm 56:11)

> *Those who live in the shelter of the Most High will find rest in the shadow of the Almighty. This I declare about the Lord: He alone is my refuge, my place of safety; he is my God, and I trust him* (Psalm 91:1-2).

REFLECT: SEEING THE INVISIBLE

(Remember to circle, underline, or otherwise highlight any words or images that stand out to you in the devotional or the related Scriptures. Include them in your journaling response.)

God desires that you experience His personal Presence and that you come to a secure rest in Him. When do you know that you know that you know God is with you?

RESPOND

Sit quietly with Jesus and simply allow Him to make you mindful of His Presence with you. Journal your reflections here.

How will I make this visible through my life today?

39

THE MORE WE SAY YES TO JESUS CHRIST, THE MORE WE GROW TO BE LIKE HIM

READ

He wants us to grow in grace, to grow in knowledge, intimacy, and fellowship with the Lord Jesus so that we will have greater zeal and steadfastness of commitment to Him with each passing day. The more we say yes to Him, the more we experience the acceleration of spiritual growth. The softer your heart is before God, the greater the acceleration of His will becomes in your life. When we are soft before Him, we are prime candidates for His manifest Presence. God wants what He is doing in each individual heart to be accelerated. He wants an acceleration of His will in our lives. It is important to note, however, that this acceleration comes from Him; it cannot be produced in the flesh. When our foot presses the accelerator of a car, the engine takes over and the vehicle's speed increases. Similarly, when we respond to God by opening our hearts, His power takes over, propelling us in the direction of greater spiritual growth (*Manifest Presence*, 66).

Further Evidence

And I will give them singleness of heart and put a new spirit within them. I will take away their stony, stubborn heart and give them a tender, responsive heart, so they will obey my decrees and regulations. Then they will truly be my people, and I will be their God (Ezekiel 11:19-20).

And this is the way to have eternal life—to know you, the only true God, and Jesus Christ, the one you sent to earth (John 17:3).

May God give you more and more grace and peace as you grow in your knowledge of God and Jesus our Lord (2 Peter 1:2).

REFLECT: SEEING THE INVISIBLE

(Remember to circle, underline, or otherwise highlight any words or images that stand out to you in the devotional or the related Scriptures. Include them in your journaling response.)

Considering the devotional paragraph above, it is God who must power our lives, not mere abilities we may have. Who is powering your life? Reflect on facets of your life where you are trying to make it on your own and invite the Presence and power of God there.

RESPOND

Quiet yourself in the Presence of Jesus and journal your reflections here.

How will I make this visible through my life today?

....

....

....

....

....

....

....

....

....

....

....

....

....

....

....

....

40

OUR HEARTS ARE BECOMING THE HOLY GROUND WHERE GOD LIVES

READ

When I do something in the name of Jesus, in effect, I'm saying, "If Jesus were here, He'd be doing the same thing." When I say, "In Jesus' name," I'm saying Jesus would do the same thing. But would He? Would He be doing those things? It's the same principle He used when He said that He never did anything unless He saw His Father in Heaven doing it (see John 8:28). Whatever He saw His Father in Heaven doing, that's what He did. In a similar vein, Matthew wrote, "People who have pure hearts are happy because they will see God" (see Matt. 5:8). Do you want to see the Lord? John said, "Anyone who has this hope [the hope of seeing the Lord Jesus] purifies himself, even as He is pure." Who wants to see God? It continues to be a matter of heart, doesn't it? A *pure* heart because my heart is His sanctuary. Whenever I am ministering from my heart, from the love, from the compassion, from the joy, from the desire that God put within me, I am beginning to minister from His fullness. And when my heart is pure and there's no brackishness there, then His life is free to flow through me. I can let loose and move with His passion (*Manifest Presence*, 69).

Further Evidence

> *So Jesus said, "When you have lifted up the Son of Man on the cross, then you will understand that I AM he. I do nothing on my own but say only what the Father taught me. And the one who sent me is with me—he has not deserted me. For I always do what pleases him"* (John 8:28-29).

> *For in him we live and move and exist* (Acts 17:28).

> *See how very much our Father loves us, for he calls us his children, and that is what we are! But the people who belong to this world don't recognize that we are God's children because they don't know him* (1 John 3:1).

REFLECT: SEEING THE INVISIBLE

(Remember to circle, underline, or otherwise highlight any words or images that stand out to you in the devotional or the related Scriptures. Include them in your journaling response.)

God is making your life more and more His holy ground. Ask the Holy Spirit to help you find and take out the trash that gets in God's way of making us His holy ground.

RESPOND

Journal here about those items that the Sprit is removing from your life today.

How will I make this visible through my life today?

....

....

....

....

....

....

....

....

....

....

....

....

....

....

....

....

....

....

....

41

WE MINISTER OUT OF HEARTS THAT ARE INHABITED BY GOD

READ

I don't think we can ever become too spiritual. When we become spiritual we become like Enoch, who walked with God and "was not." He was just translated. Until we are translated, we can be as spiritual as we need to be. The requirements the Holy Spirit puts on us are not beyond our ability. We need to be soft and flexible and allow the purity of the Lord to flow through us. We are called to be people who can minister from our hearts. If our hearts are hard or angry or bitter or hurt, we cannot minister from the sanctuary because those things close us off from a place of purity within. God wants us to minister in purity from the sanctuary of our hearts, whether it's to an individual or through preaching, or if it's officiating at marriages or pastoring people or prophesying or whatever it is we're doing. There is a deeper relationship with God that we can experience if we open our hearts to His manifest Presence (*Manifest Presence*, 72-73).

Further Evidence

> *Enoch lived 365 years, walking in close fellowship with God. Then one day he disappeared, because God took him (Genesis 5:23-24).*

> *A good person produces good things from the treasury of a good heart, and an evil person produces evil things from the treasury of an evil heart. What you say flows from what is in your heart (Luke 6:45).*

> *Anyone who believes in me may come and drink! For the Scriptures declare, "Rivers of living water will flow from his heart" (John 7:38).*

REFLECT: SEEING THE INVISIBLE

(Remember to circle, underline, or otherwise highlight any words or images that stand out to you in the devotional or the related Scriptures. Include them in your journaling response.)

What you carry in your heart becomes the basis of how you live and respond to God in the world. Are there areas in our hearts that need to be healed and unloaded? Ask Jesus in a quiet place to reveal what needs to be healed in your heart.

RESPOND

Reflect and journal what Jesus speaks into those areas of woundedness.

How will I make this visible in my life today?

42

MAKING ROOM SO JESUS CHRIST CAN REIGN THROUGH US

READ

Jesus has never wanted to come just to visit. He has always wanted to come to stay, to dwell permanently so that revival would be an intense, continual experience of His Presence that grows greater and greater and greater. For Him to take up permanent residence in my life, in my fellowship, in my ministry, in my town, means His Lordship ruling and reigning over me and over all that He has given me to care for. That means a radical alteration of my plans, a radical alteration of how I conduct my business, because Jesus has come to stay. And when He comes to stay, everything changes—permanently (*Manifest Presence*, 86).

Further Evidence

> *Many plans are in a man's heart, but the counsel of the Lord will stand* (Proverbs 19:21 NASB).

In the last days, this is what is going to happen: The hill upon which the Always-Present One's temple stands will become the most important of all hills. It will be raised above the other hills. Various peoples will flow to it. Many nations will come and say: "Come, let us go up to the mountain of the Always-Present One, and to the temple of the God of Jacob! Then God will teach us from His ways. And, we will live by His paths." (Micah 4:1-2 PEB).

He [Jesus] walked away, about a stone's throw, and knelt down and prayed, "Father, if you are willing, please take this cup of suffering away from me. Yet I want your will to be done, not mine" (Luke 22:41-42).

REFLECT: SEEING THE INVISIBLE

(Remember to circle, underline, or otherwise highlight any words or images that stand out to you in the devotional or the related Scriptures. Include them in your journaling response.)

When Jesus moves in, our agenda moves out. How much of your human will governs your life? Reflect on this question here. Where does Jesus desire to move in your life in this next season?

RESPOND

Journal here about new areas where Jesus is moving into your life.

How will I make this visible through my life today?

....

....

....

....

....

....

....

....

....

....

....

....

....

....

....

....

....

....

....

43

WE ARE THE HOLY PLACE OF GOD'S HABITATION

READ

God wants His Tabernacle to be among humankind. The Scriptures say, "God's sanctuary is among human beings" (see Rev. 21:3). The word *Emmanuel* means "God with us." His intention was never to communicate to us from afar, but to dwell in our hearts from a place of permanent intimacy. *"The Always-Present One has chosen Jerusalem"* (Ps. 132:13 PEB). He wants to live there *perpetually*. What excitement there is in knowing that God's permanent residence is inside you and me. His permanent residence is in the Church. When God comes in, everything He is and everything He has comes with Him. That requires everything that is out of harmony with God to change (*Manifest Presence*, 88).

Further Evidence

The high and lofty one who lives in eternity, the Holy One, says this: "I live in the high and holy place with those whose spirits are contrite and humble. I restore the crushed spirit of the humble and revive the courage of those with repentant hearts" (Isaiah 57:15).

Look! The virgin will conceive a child! She will give birth to a son, and they will call him Immanuel, which means "God is with us" (Matthew 1:23).

Jesus replied, "All who love me will do what I say. My Father will love them, and we will come and make our home with each of them" (John 14:23).

REFLECT: SEEING THE INVISIBLE

(Remember to circle, underline, or otherwise highlight any words or images that stand out to you in the devotional or the related Scriptures. Include them in your journaling response.)

When Jesus Christ moved into your heart He brought His Kingdom's power and priorities with Him. You are a subject of that Kingdom. Allow His Kingdom to grow in you.

RESPOND

Reflect and journal on what new priorities Jesus might be bringing into your life in this season.

How will I make this visible through my life today?

44

THE FIRST CASUALTY ON THE SPIRITUAL CUTTING EDGE IS US!

READ

If we're to be on the cutting edge of what God is doing in this hour, if we want to be those who will be manifesting His Presence throughout the earth, we have to allow everything we have ever thought, hoped, believed, or felt to be placed on the altar of God. This does not necessarily mean that God will sacrifice it all. All too frequently, however, people consider God to be their spiritual smorgasbord—they can pick and choose whatever they want from God. The truth is, however, that we are His smorgasbord—we are to be laid upon the altar where He can pick and choose what He wants of us! There are many folks who are excited about being on the cutting edge of what God is doing. Many want to be in the center of God's will and be found doing what is pleasing to Him. But few folks realize that to be on the cutting edge of what God is doing means that God has to be on the cutting edge of our hearts. We have to allow Him to cut and mold and make us into His image and into His likeness. That's what the cutting edge is all about. God's cutting edge is at work in my life (*Manifest Presence*, 106).

Further Evidence

> *Then the Lord gave me this message: "O Israel, can I not do to you as this potter has done to his clay? As the clay is in the potter's hand, so are you in my hand"* (Jeremiah 18:5-6).

> *And so, dear brothers and sisters, I plead with you to give your bodies to God because of all he has done for you. Let them be a living and holy sacrifice—the kind he will find acceptable* (Romans 12:1).

> *And you are living stones that God is building into his spiritual temple. What's more, you are his holy priests* (1 Peter 2:5).

REFLECT: SEEING THE INVISIBLE

(Remember to circle, underline, or otherwise highlight any words or images that stand out to you in the devotional or the related Scriptures. Include them in your journaling response.)

God is molding you into His purpose and likeness. When do you try to crawl off the Potter's wheel? Reflect on how the hand of God has been molding and making you more like Himself.

RESPONSE

Journal your response as you sit quietly with Jesus.
How will I make this visible through my life today?

45

GOD IS WITH US EVERY STEP OF THE JOURNEY

READ

In your darkest times, when God's voice seems nonexistent and His Presence is nowhere to be found, He is still there. Not only is He still there, He is still working on your behalf and on behalf of your family and those around you. Elisha cried out, "Lord, give him eyes to see what I see!" (see 2 Kings 6:17). The mountains were filled with the armies of the Lord. Lord, give *me* eyes to see what You are doing around me. May my spiritual perception grow and develop that I might be able to see Your hand of mercy, healing, restoration, guidance, love, and persistence on a moment-by-moment basis.

I'm not going to pretend to tell you that I know why God's Presence seems so distant at times. Sometimes it feels as though He has lifted His hands from us. But I can say with certainty that His ways are not our ways. He will never leave us or forsake us. As Moses declared so many years ago to the children of Israel, *"He brought us out from there in order to bring us in, to give us the land which He had sworn to our fathers"* (Deut. 6:23 NASB). God doesn't change His mind halfway through a plan. He does not give up, quit, or take a holiday. We do those things, but He does not. Ever (*Supernatural Destiny*, 155-156).

Further Evidence

> *So be strong and courageous! Do not be afraid and do not panic before them. For the Lord your God will personally go ahead of you. He will neither fail you nor abandon you* (Deuteronomy 31:6).

> *The Lord is close to the brokenhearted; he rescues those whose spirits are crushed* (Psalm 34:18).

> *He will feed his flock like a shepherd. He will carry the lambs in his arms, holding them close to his heart. He will gently lead the mother sheep with their young* (Isaiah 40:11).

REFLECT: SEEING THE INVISIBLE

(Remember to circle, underline, or otherwise highlight any words or images that stand out to you in the devotional or the related Scriptures. Include them in your journaling response.)

God never changes His mind about us. He is with us every step of the journey, whether we feel it or not. Sometimes, when God feels far away from you, you may convict Him of abandonment. He is still here even when we don't *feel* His Presence. Take time to pray as Elisha did, "Lord give me eyes to see."

RESPONSE

Think about times and places where you have not felt God's Presence. Journal your reflections here.

How will I make this visible through my life today?

....

....

....

....

....

....

....

....

....

....

....

....

....

....

....

....

....

....

....

....

....

....

....

....

46

GOD WILL NOT BE KEPT AT A SAFE DISTANCE; HE IS NEAR

READ

The nearness of God is not a flippant experience, nor is it safe for the deceptive of heart. His reality within changes everything. He is suddenly not a philosophy, not a doctrine or a belief system. Suddenly, and I do mean suddenly, He is the living Creator God who has come to dwell within the human heart—yours and mine. Ancient Israel was happy to have God on Mount Sinai. He was far away from those who called Him God. They did not have to deal with the immediacy of His Presence. He was a safe distance for their human antics. But David brought the Presence back to the people. He pitched a tent, as it were, in his backyard for the Presence of the King to dwell. The Divine was now there, near, immediate (*Forgotten Mountain*, 25-26).

Further Evidence

> *For the Lord declares, "I have placed my chosen king on the throne in Jerusalem, on my holy mountain"* (Psalm 2:6).

But as for me, how good it is to be near God! I have made the Sovereign Lord my shelter, and I will tell everyone about the wonderful things you do (Psalm 73:28).

REFLECT: SEEING THE INVISIBLE

(Remember to circle, underline, or otherwise highlight any words or images that stand out to you in the devotional or the related Scriptures. Include them in your journaling response.)

God's Presence in your life demands a response just as any other person's Presence would. Your response requires, first, an acknowledgement of God's Presence. As you sit quietly, consider how you might acknowledge God's Presence throughout the day. Even right at this very moment.

RESPOND

Acknowledge the Presence of God in your journaling here. How will I make this visible through my life today?

....

....

....

....

....

....

....

47

GOD LIVES IN US AND THROUGH US AS WE CARRY HIS PRESENCE

READ

His [God's] Presence is not a gift; it is the result of Divine desire and is the product of broken repentance. These folks [those who minister as priests of the Presence of God] understand that they have nothing to give if they do not give Him who is within. They have discovered that reducing their faith to a mere philosophy reduces their Redeemer to the level of other social experiments and puts them on a level playing field with all others who vie for the attention of humanity. The difference between this priesthood and other methods is that they actually serve and dwell in the Presence of the living God. This living God also lives within them. This reality cannot be overstated and cannot be dismissed. He Himself is the Divine King who is on a mission of His own. That mission is to bring the tranquil, compassionate, healing atmosphere of Heaven into time and space (*Forgotten Mountain*, 92).

Further Evidence

I have given them the glory you gave me, so they may be one as we are one. I am in them and you are in me. May they experience such perfect unity that the world will know that you sent me and that you love them as much as you love me (John 17:22-23).

But you will receive power when the Holy Spirit comes upon you. And you will be my witnesses, telling people about me everywhere—in Jerusalem, throughout Judea, in Samaria, and to the ends of the earth (Acts 1:8).

And as we live in God, our love grows more perfect. So we will not be afraid on the day of judgment, but we can face him with confidence because we live like Jesus here in this world (1 John 4:17).

REFLECT: SEEING THE INVISIBLE

(Remember to circle, underline, or otherwise highlight any words or images that stand out to you in the devotional or the related Scriptures. Include them in your journaling response.)

God is not a theory or philosophy; He is real and He is present in and through you. How does your life represent the Presence of God to those who live around you?

RESPOND

Reflect and journal here on the Lord living through you to your friends, family, employer, and faith community. Be specific.

How will I make this visible through my life today?

48

As We Carry His Presence We Are Changed and Change the World Around Us

Read

The work that the King is doing [in and through us] cannot be duplicated. It cannot be manufactured by human understanding. I will say it again. The absolute reality of His manifest Presence cannot be faked. The union of word and demonstration of His life in the individual will change the world because it changes individuals. Those who are given to Him have no personal agenda, no political ideology, and no desire for personal fame. They are indwelled by Him, changed by Him, led by Him. They live in surrendered brokenness, and their joy is to see Him exalted among humanity (*Forgotten Mountain*, 95).

Further Evidence

> *This message was kept secret for centuries and generations past, but now it has been revealed to God's people.*

For God wanted them to know that the riches and glory of Christ are for you Gentiles, too. And this is the secret: Christ lives in you. This gives you assurance of sharing his glory (Colossians 1:26-27).

For all who are led by the Spirit of God are children of God (Romans 8:14).

And because we are his children, God has sent the Spirit of his Son into our hearts, prompting us to call out, "Abba, Father" (Galatians 4:6).

REFLECT: SEEING THE INVISIBLE

(Remember to circle, underline, or otherwise highlight any words or images that stand out to you in the devotional or the related Scriptures. Include them in your journaling response.)

You *re-present* Christ as He lives in and through you in a broken world. Let's take time to reexamine what is most important to us. Expand your reflections from the previous journal entries. How does your life represent the life of the King within you to people you may not even know?

RESPOND

Journal here concerning how people you don't really know may see Jesus through your life.

How will I make this visible through my life today?

49

THE PRESENCE OF GOD IN OUR LIVES ANNOUNCES THE ARRIVAL OF HIS KINGDOM TO THE WORLD

READ

His [God's] mighty love arises within His people. He is sovereign. He is engaged. He is consuming. His Presence shuts the mouths of His detractors. This Kingdom and this King will not be marginalized either by political expediency or religious ecumenism. His Kingdom is established in the heart or it is not established at all. His reign is not from the top down. It is from the inside out. He wins the hearts of nations one heart at a time. He works through everyday folks who have committed to allow His simple reign within. In the "yes" of the King, they are true instruments of change, for their radical commitment to inner transformation reflects the Person of the King and His relentless love for this planet. The language of this union, this priesthood is the language of true love—true, unconditional love. It is a love that gathers those so many others ignore, heals those who are the outcasts, and loves those who have never felt or experienced the reality of true love. True Divine love is evident to those who are governed by the King (*Forgotten Mountain*, 95-96).

Further Evidence

> *Don't you realize that your body is the temple of the Holy Spirit, who lives in you and was given to you by God? You do not belong to yourself* (1 Corinthians 6:19).

> *Don't you realize that all of you together are the temple of God and that the Spirit of God lives in you?* (1 Corinthians 3:16)

> *For we are the temple of the living God. As God said: "I will live in them and walk among them. I will be their God, and they will be my people"* (2 Corinthians 6:16).

REFLECT: SEEING THE INVISIBLE

(Remember to circle, underline, or otherwise highlight any words or images that stand out to you in the devotional or the related Scriptures. Include them in your journaling response.)

All change in God begins on the inside and becomes evident on the outside. Invite the Spirit to build His temple in you. Settle into the Presence of Jesus and reflect on what the Spirit wants to deal with in your life that is not vital to His purpose of making you His temple.

RESPOND

Journal here regarding what you see the Spirit clearing out of His temple, your life.

How will I make this visible through my life today?

....

....

....

....

....

....

....

....

....

....

....

....

....

....

....

....

....

50

CHRIST BRINGS US BACK INTO HIS PRESENCE WHERE WE ARE RENEWED

READ

When God sent the King [Jesus Christ] to the earth, He sent the King to redeem mankind so the law would be fulfilled. In short, He gave all men the possibility to be priests to God. He forgave their sin, cleansed them from their penchant toward sin, filled them with the Presence of the King for the purpose of changing the heart of man so that they would, by nature, surrender themselves to God. Because of what the King accomplished on the earth, all men could now not only approach God but have fellowship with Him. Not because man was perfect but because he was redeemed from the consequences of the law. Now man could approach God with confidence knowing that the blood of the King covered man's imperfection until the power and love of the King was able to change him. By presenting themselves to the King for inner transformation and governance, man would be empowered and changed by the very Presence of the King within (*Forgotten Mountain*, 106).

Further Evidence

> *How precious is your unfailing love, O God! All humanity finds shelter in the shadow of your wings* (Psalm 36:7).

> *So you also should consider yourselves to be dead to the power of sin and alive to God through Christ Jesus* (Romans 6:11).

> *Instead, be kind to each other, tenderhearted, forgiving one another, just as God through Christ has forgiven you* (Ephesians 4:32).

REFLECT: SEEING THE INVISIBLE

(Remember to circle, underline, or otherwise highlight any words or images that stand out to you in the devotional or the related Scriptures. Include them in your journaling response.)

Imagine that you are invited into the very throne room of God. How would standing in His throne room change and transform you? Sit quietly in His Presence now and visualize walking into His throne room.

RESPOND

How would this change or transform your life? Journal your response here.

How will I make this visible through my life today?

51

GOD'S PRESENCE BECOMES VISIBLE THROUGH HIS CHURCH

READ

God will so fill the Church with His manifest Presence that He will become perceptible (i.e. tangible) to any or all of our five senses. God manifests Himself in healing. God manifests Himself in change. God manifests Himself in restoration. God manifests Himself in prophecy. Whenever God manifests Himself through any of our natural senses, there is always a visible demonstration that He is literally in the midst of His people (*Manifest Presence*, 21).

Further Evidence

> *I will make my home among them. I will be their God, and they will be my people. And when my Temple is among them forever, the nations will know that I am the Lord, who makes Israel holy* (Ezekiel 37:27-28).

Jesus replied, "All who love me will do what I say. My Father will love them, and we will come and make our home with each of them" (John 14:23).

For ever since the world was created, people have seen the earth and sky. Through everything God made, they can clearly see his invisible qualities—his eternal power and divine nature. So they have no excuse for not knowing God (Romans 1:20).

REFLECT: SEEING THE INVISIBLE

(Remember to circle, underline, or otherwise highlight any words or images that stand out to you in the devotional or the related Scriptures. Include them in your journaling response.)

God desires to make Himself real to you personally. God is with us personally as we make ourselves mindful of His Presence. As you quiet yourself in the Presence of God, make yourself aware of His Presence through your five senses.

RESPOND

Journal here regarding how you might experience God with what you see, hear, smell, or feel.

How will I make this visible through my life today?

52

GOD DESIRES TO MAKE HIMSELF TANGIBLE TO US

READ

The dictionary defines *manifest* as "readily perceived by the senses; easily understood or recognized by the mind; obvious." This is how God wants to make Himself known to us in these last days. God manifested Himself in the midst of His people. It was not an unusual thing to them; it was actually quite common. All the nations of the world had their gods, but Israel was unique in that their God dwelt with them. All the nations of the world would look at Israel and tremble because the God they served was manifested among them. They saw Him; they knew Him. God was in the midst of the children of Israel. It was God's manifest Presence in the burning bush on that powerful day when Moses was commissioned to be Israel's deliverer. So mighty was His Presence that God commanded Moses to remove his sandals. "For," the Scriptures declare, "the place where you are standing is holy ground" (Exod. 3:5 NIV) (*Manifest Presence*, 21,23).

Further Evidence

> *Then Moses said, "If you don't personally go with us, don't make us leave this place. How will anyone know that you look favorably on me—on me and on your people—if you don't go with us? For your presence among us sets your people and me apart from all other people on the earth"* (Exodus 33:15-16).

> *You must be holy because I, the Lord, am holy. I have set you apart from all other people to be my very own* (Leviticus 20:26).

> *So now I am giving you a new commandment: Love each other. Just as I have loved you, you should love each other. Your love for one another will prove to the world that you are my disciples* (John 13:34-35).

REFLECT: SEEING THE INVISIBLE

(Remember to circle, underline, or otherwise highlight any words or images that stand out to you in the devotional or the related Scriptures. Include them in your journaling response.)

Your life is holy ground. God desires to lead you by the Spirit in every area of your life. In the quiet Presence of Jesus, reflect on some kind of burning bush experience you've had with the Presence of God (as Moses in Exodus 3).

RESPOND

Write about your burning bush experiences here.

How will I make this visible through my life today?

....

....

....

....

....

....

....

....

....

....

....

....

....

....

....

....

....

....

....

....

53

GOD DESIRES THAT WE EXPERIENCE HIS PRESENCE AND POWER

READ

In our day, we are beginning to see a continual fulfilling of Emmanuel—God with us. God has always desired to live and dwell and manifest Himself in the midst of His people. As He walked with Adam in the cool of the evening (see Gen. 3:8), God also wants to walk with us, so that we will become a people who will experience His Presence, His power, and His glory in a tangible way. The days directly ahead of us will require this. Periods of tribulation and hardship have always driven the people of God into His Presence, thus experiencing His power in mighty ways. Difficult times press God's people into Him so that they, too, will experience His Manifest Presence (*Manifest Presence*, 27).

Further Evidence

> *I will bless the Lord who guides me; even at night my heart instructs me. I know the Lord is always with me. I will not be shaken, for he is right beside me* (Psalm 16:7-8).

The Lord is a friend to those who fear him. He teaches them his covenant (Psalm 25:14).

I no longer call you slaves, because a master doesn't confide in his slaves. Now you are my friends, since I have told you everything the Father told me (John 15:15).

REFLECT: SEEING THE INVISIBLE

(Remember to circle, underline, or otherwise highlight any words or images that stand out to you in the devotional or the related Scriptures. Include them in your journaling response.)

God in Jesus Christ is making you part of His plan for planet earth. Considering your life experiences and personality, how do you see yourself as part of His plan?

RESPOND

Journal about your friendship with God and your part in His plan.

How will I make this visible through my life today?

54

GOD WANTS TO BE PART OF OUR EVERYDAY LIVES

READ

In our day, we are beginning to see a continual fulfilling of Emmanuel—God with us. God has always desired to live and dwell and manifest Himself in the midst of His people. As He walked with Adam in the cool of the evening (see Gen. 3:8), God also wants to walk with us, so that we will become a people who will experience His Presence, His power, and His glory in a tangible way. The days directly ahead of us will require this. Periods of tribulation and hardship have always driven the people of God into His Presence, thus experiencing His power in mighty ways. Difficult times press God's people into Him so that they, too, will experience His manifest Presence (*Manifest Presence*, 27).

Further Evidence

> *Here on earth you will have many trials and sorrows. But take heart, because I have overcome the world* (John 16:33).

Dear brothers and sisters, when troubles of any kind come your way, consider it an opportunity for great joy. For you know that when your faith is tested, your endurance has a chance to grow. So let it grow, for when your endurance is fully developed, you will be perfect and complete, needing nothing (James 1:2-4).

So be truly glad. There is wonderful joy ahead, even though you have to endure many trials for a little while. These trials will show that your faith is genuine. It is being tested as fire tests and purifies gold—though your faith is far more precious than mere gold. So when your faith remains strong through many trials, it will bring you much praise and glory and honor on the day when Jesus Christ is revealed to the whole world (1 Peter 1:6-7).

REFLECT: SEEING THE INVISIBLE

(Remember to circle, underline, or otherwise highlight any words or images that stand out to you in the devotional or the related Scriptures. Include them in your journaling response.)

God is with you regardless of circumstance. He redeems and fills your valleys with praise. Can you think of times when God has redeemed a challenging time and filled it with His Presence? What does this say about the heart of God?

RESPOND

Journal about God's redeeming of a challenging time in your life and what that says about the heart of God.

How will I make this visible through my life today?

THE WORLD KNOWS
THE PRESENCE OF GOD
THROUGH HIS PEOPLE

READ

We're living in a time of great excitement and great anticipation. God is about to move upon us. Just as God manifested
Himself in the days of Israel, so He wants to manifest Himself
today in reality. *"Arise, Jerusalem! Let your light shine for all to
see. The splendor of the Always-Present One shines on you"* (Isa.
60:1 PEB). When the glory of the Lord rises upon the Church,
it will be visible. People will know that God is in the midst of
His people. *"For behold, darkness will cover the earth and deep
darkness the peoples; but the Lord will rise upon you and His
glory will appear upon you. Nations will come to your light, and
kings to the brightness of your rising"* (Isa. 60:2-3 NASB) (*Manifest Presence*, 40).

Further Evidence

> *For you have rescued me from death; you have kept my feet from slipping. So now I can walk in your presence, O God, in your life-giving light* (Psalm 56:13).

> *Arise, Jerusalem! Let your light shine for all to see. For the glory of the Lord rises to shine on you* (Isaiah 60:1).

> *Jesus spoke to the people once more and said, "I am the light of the world. If you follow me, you won't have to walk in darkness, because you will have the light that leads to life"* (John 8:12).

> *But while I am here in the world, I am the light of the world* (John 9:5).

REFLECT: SEEING THE INVISIBLE

Jesus is the Light of the world. Light allows us to see things clearly. How does that Light illuminate your path? Take time in the Presence of Jesus to reflect on how that Light makes a difference in your daily life.

RESPOND

Journal here about how the Presence of Jesus in your life allows you to see life more clearly.

How will I make this visible through my life today?

The World Knows the Presence of God Through His People

56

GOD CALLS US TO WALK WITH HIM MOMENT BY MOMENT

READ

We will need to experience the miraculous power of God moment by moment. That will come only through an abiding, intimate relationship with Him. These are the days when we must seek the Lord while He may be found, when we must conform to His will and His desires and allow His Spirit to change us from glory to glory, so that we will be able to stand in the days ahead. Our only hope for revival, for restoration, for an outpouring of the Holy Spirit is for God to establish His glory among His people. When His glory rises in the Church, there will be a people who will simply respond to Him by saying, "God, do whatever You want to do." God's people won't argue with Him. They won't be bound by their own traditions and pet doctrines. They're not going to hold their own opinions so dear that God will not be able to speak to them (*Manifest Presence*, 41-42).

Further Evidence

> *The Lord continued, "Look, stand near me on this rock"* (Exodus 33:21).

> *Those who live in the shelter of the Most High will find rest in the shadow of the Almighty* (Psalm 91:1).

> *I wait quietly before God, for my victory comes from him. He alone is my rock and my salvation, my fortress where I will never be shaken* (Psalm 62:1-2).

> *My people will live in safety, quietly at home. They will be at rest* (Isaiah 32:18).

REFLECT: SEEING THE INVISIBLE

(Remember to circle, underline, or otherwise highlight any words or images that stand out to you in the devotional or the related Scriptures. Include them in your journaling response.)

The Lord transforms you moment by moment as you seek Him. Be present to God by shifting your attention away from your circumstances and onto Him in this moment.

RESPOND

Take time to write your response here as you shift your focus away from your circumstances and onto God's Presence in this moment.

How will I make this visible through my life today?

57

WE ARE PRIESTS OF THE PRESENCE OF GOD

READ

You are the priests of the Presence. You are the royal priest-hood, the holy nation. You are already the ministers of His glory whether or not you are ever recognized or ordained by anyone. He has seen you, recognized you, and called you to Himself. You may never stand in a pulpit or teach a Sunday school class, but you minister His Presence because He lives in you. The dream God has dreamed for mankind can only be fulfilled when we all step forward and become everything that He has placed in our hearts to be as individuals. Many of us are waiting for the opportunity, the possibility of inti-mate fellowship, friendship, and service to our Lord that will last for the rest of our lives. You are the ones who understand that you are priests of the Presence. You are God's intended instrument of mercy, love, and salvation. You are the lamp in whom dwells the Light of the World (*Secrets of the Most Holy Place*, 14-15).

Further Evidence

And you will be my kingdom of priests, my holy nation (Exodus 19:6).

And so, dear brothers and sisters, I plead with you to give your bodies to God because of all he has done for you. Let them be a living and holy sacrifice—the kind he will find acceptable. This is truly the way to worship him (Romans 12:1).

And you have caused them to become a Kingdom of priests for our God. And they will reign on the earth (Revelation 5:10).

And you are living stones that God is building into his spiritual temple. What's more, you are his holy priests. Through the mediation of Jesus Christ, you offer spiritual sacrifices that please God (1 Peter 2:5).

REFLECT: SEEING THE INVISIBLE

(Remember to circle, underline, or otherwise highlight any words or images that stand out to you in the devotional or the related Scriptures. Include them in your journaling response.)

As a priest of God's Presence you *re-present* God to man and man to God. Allow God to clothe you with the garments of His Presence now. Your garments are humility and your sacrifice is obedience.

RESPOND

Journal about taking on your priestly garments and fulfilling your office in the Presence of Jesus, our High Priest.

How will I make this visible through my life today?

....

....

....

....

....

....

....

....

....

....

....

....

....

....

....

....

....

58

THE PRESENCE OF GOD IS LIKE A RIVER FLOWING THROUGH US

READ

The river of God's Presence is the river of God inside, and it is always flowing. It doesn't really matter whether it's raining or not. The river is there because of the spring rain and is flowing within. This river flows through me all summer to the time of the latter, harvest rain. Since we have His Presence with us, it is always oozing from us like an artesian well. Our lips can always flow with milk and honey to nourish a dying planet. For this flow is not dependent upon my mood or my attitude. It does not hinge upon whether I remembered to do all the "right" things. The river within is not dependent upon me; it flows because it has a life and destiny of its own. I have become a living prayer before the Lord to the nations, always open, always ready to hear, always ready to obey (*Secrets of the Most Holy Place*, 71).

Further Evidence

There is a river whose streams make glad the city of God, the holy place where the Most High dwells (Psalm 46:4 NIV).

Jesus replied, "If you only knew the gift God has for you and who you are speaking to, you would ask me, and I would give you living water" (John 4:10).

Anyone who believes in me may come and drink! For the Scriptures declare, "Rivers of living water will flow from his heart" (John 7:38).

REFLECT: SEEING THE INVISIBLE

(Remember to circle, underline, or otherwise highlight any words or images that stand out to you in the devotional or the related Scriptures. Include them in your journaling response.)

As you grow in your awareness of the Presence of God you become a well from which the world can drink, particularly through your words. How do the words that you yourself speak provide a flow of living water to the world?

RESPOND

Journal here asking Jesus to help you recognize the source of your own words.

How will I make this visible through my life today?

IN THE PRESENCE OF THE LORD WE FIND STRENGTH FOR THE JOURNEY

READ

(A prayer) Lord, I'm so tired. I just can't do this anymore. When I say those words, I can hear Your response, Lord: "That's right. You can't. Now, will you let Me?" I guess that's exactly what You meant when You said, *"My strength is made perfect in weakness."* I really won't experience Your strength until I reach the end of my own. Well, I've reached that end, Lord. I'm worn out and tired. My heart is so overwhelmed that I can't even find my way to You. So please lead me. Lead me into Your Presence and wash away my weariness. I stand here before You, and I lift my hands. I need You, Jesus. I cannot go another step until You strengthen me. Here, from the end of the earth, I cry out to You! Strengthen my heart! Strengthen my body! Strengthen my mind! Strengthen my love for You! Amen (*Hope for a Praying Nation*, 115-116).

Further Evidence

> *He gives power to the weak and strength to the powerless. Even youths will become weak and tired, and young men will fall in exhaustion. But those who trust in the Lord will find new strength. They will soar high on wings like eagles. They will run and not grow weary. They will walk and not faint* (Isaiah 40:29-31).

> *For I have given rest to the weary and joy to the sorrowing* (Jeremiah 31:25).

> *"My grace is all you need. My power works best in weakness." So now I am glad to boast about my weaknesses, so that the power of Christ can work through me* (2 Corinthians 12:9).

REFLECT: SEEING THE INVISIBLE

(Remember to circle, underline, or otherwise highlight any words or images that stand out to you in the devotional or the related Scriptures. Include them in your journaling response.)

When you are weary and overwhelmed, God is only a whisper away. Give Him your weakness now and find His strength. Ask Jesus to exchange your weakness for His strength.

RESPOND

As you journal, bring to mind aspects of your life that feel overwhelming to you. Write Jesus' response here.

How will I make this visible through my life today?

In the Presence of the Lord We Find Strength for the Journey

60

GOD IS NOT INTERESTED IN A TEMPORARY VISIT WITH US; HE WANTS TO MOVE IN

READ

A visitation from the Lord is just like a weekend with the grandparents. We never plan for a visitation from God to turn into anything permanent. That's probably why visitation is just that—a visitation. It's easy to say that He comes for a season and then, for whatever sovereign reason deep in God's heart, He leaves. But God never intended to visit us. He has always planned to stay. It is only our man-made doctrines of visitation that justify the fact that the Presence of God does not abide among us. So here is the secret. If you only want a visitation, then plan for a visitation. But if you hunger for the permanent restoration of God's manifest Presence among His people, plan for Him to stay. Prepare for Him. Expect Him. Welcome Him. Yield to Him. Continuously make room in your heart for Him. He will come. He will come to stay (*Secrets of the Most Holy Place*, 91-92).

Further Evidence

> *O Jerusalem, Jerusalem, the city that kills the prophets and stones God's messengers! How often I have wanted to gather your children together as a hen protects her chicks beneath her wings, but you wouldn't let me* (Matthew 23:37).

> *Jesus replied, "All who love me will do what I say. My Father will love them, and we will come and make our home with each of them"* (John 14:23).

> *As God said, "I will live in them and walk among them. I will be their God, and they will be my people"* (2 Corinthians 6:16).

REFLECT: SEEING THE INVISIBLE

(Remember to circle, underline, or otherwise highlight any words or images that stand out to you in the devotional or the related Scriptures. Include them in your journaling response.)

Have you given God the keys to your house, so to speak? He wants to be more than an occasional visitor. Prepare for Him. Make room for Him. In the quiet Presence of Jesus, ask Him what needs to be moved out so that He can move in in order for Him to take up residence in your heart.

RESPOND

Write about making room for Jesus in your heart here. How will I make this visible through my life today?

FINDING YOUR
PURPOSE IN GOD

61

OUR PURPOSE IN LIFE IS TO LIVE AS SONS AND DAUGHTERS OF GOD

READ

"I am a son" is a statement of identity and of life. It is a declaration of destiny and empowerment, of love and of confidence. No testimony can be greater than the realization that above all else in life, I am a son! That four-word declaration changes everything. It changes everything, that is, if I have experienced Him as my Father in the crucible of gritty circumstances and difficult people—the crucible of uncertainty and loneliness, loss and fear, despair and darkness. For those who are on the path of life, these are the instruments of transformational change that help us grow from a rebel son to a maturing son, from an immature son to a father. These unavoidable turns in life can certainly change us from whiners to doers, from takers to givers, from echoes to voices, from babes to kings who can co-rule with the King (*I Am a Son*, 10).

Further Evidence

> *But to all who believed him and accepted him, he gave the right to become children of God* (John 1:12).

> *For all who are led by the Spirit of God are children of God* (Romans 8:14).

> *And I will be your Father, and you will be my sons and daughters, says the Lord Almighty* (2 Corinthians 6:18).

REFLECT: SEEING THE INVISIBLE

(Remember to circle, underline, or otherwise highlight any words or images that stand out to you in the devotional or the related Scriptures. Include them in your journaling response.)

Your ultimate purpose and identity in God is that you are His child and heir to His Kingdom with Jesus Christ. What might we try to add to this core identity as God's children?

RESPOND

Take time in the Presence of God and journal what it means to you to personally be His child.

How will I make this visible through my life today?

62

WE ARE CHILDREN OF GOD REGARDLESS OF STATION, STATUS, OR CIRCUMSTANCE

READ

It is during these difficult times that I discover the unlimited power of my Father's unconditional, never-failing, always-healing love. I find Him truly, deeply in the valleys of deep, personal uncertainty. When I want to run, He runs beside me; when I want to die, He reminds me that He already did; when I want to quit, He holds me up. It is then I discover what it means to be a son of my Father who, truly, will never leave me, forsake me, or lose hope in me. I know I am a son because my Father proved Himself when I needed Him most. He never doubted, never gave up on the dream He has for me, never lost confidence that I would fulfill my destiny. This is the knowledge that a Bible school can't teach, a prophet can't declare, a worship song can't impart, and decreeing can't force. I am a son because I run to Him every day without excusing my humanity, blaming someone else, or whining over an unfair circumstance (*I Am a Son,* 11).

Further Evidence

> *It is the Lord who goes before you. He will be with you. He will not fail you or abandon you. Do not fear or be dismayed* (Deuteronomy 31:8 AMP).

> *Once I was young, and now I am old. Yet I have never seen the godly abandoned or their children begging for bread* (Psalm 37:25).

> *We know that God's children do not make a practice of sinning, for God's Son holds them securely, and the evil one cannot touch them* (1 John 5:18).

REFLECT: SEEING THE INVISIBLE

(Remember to circle, underline, or otherwise highlight any words or images that stand out to you in the devotional or the related Scriptures. Include them in your journaling response.)

The overwhelming and unlimited love of God is available to you as you claim your identity as a child of God. He will never cease to love you, nor will He leave you. Settle into the Presence of Jesus and talk to Him about areas of uncertainty in your life.

RESPOND

Acknowledge His Presence as you journal your conversation here.

How will I make this visible through my life today?

63

MATURE SONS GROW UP AND TAKE THEIR PLACE IN THE PURPOSE OF THEIR FATHER

READ

I am a son. I do not want to miss God's purpose for me or any whom I love. I must learn to face the music, dance to the song the band plays, and grow up. Mature sons inherit everything. Immature sons, prodigal sons, demand their inheritance now and destroy the future for themselves, their children, and their children's children. Maybe that is why it is so difficult to pass this vibrant faith on to the next generation? Maybe we have settled for a lesser god? Maybe we are passing on a moral code, traditions that require only an outward adherence to list of commandments that have no power to actually, generationally change lives (*I Am a Son*, 36).

Further Evidence

> A man had two sons. The younger son told his father, "I want my share of your estate now before you die." So his

father agreed to divide his wealth between his sons. A few days later this younger son packed all his belongings and moved to a distant land, and there he wasted all his money in wild living (Luke 15:11-13).

And since we are his children, we are his heirs. In fact, together with Christ we are heirs of God's glory. But if we are to share his glory, we must also share his suffering (Romans 8:17).

And now that you belong to Christ, you are the true children of Abraham. You are his heirs, and God's promise to Abraham belongs to you (Galatians 3:29).

REFLECT: SEEING THE INVISIBLE

(Remember to circle, underline, or otherwise highlight any words or images that stand out to you in the devotional or the related Scriptures. Include them in your journaling response.)

You are growing and maturing as a child and heir of God. As a maturing child you will be more and more focused on His purpose. His purpose is performed through your identity in Jesus Christ. Settle in the Presence of Jesus, the Firstborn of creation, and exchange your wants and concerns for His.

RESPOND

Journal here about Jesus' wants and concerns regarding your life.

How will I make this visible through my life today?

64

GOD INFUSED US WITH PURPOSE WHEN HE CREATED EACH ONE OF US

READ

We are neither here by accident, nor do we walk alone on this sojourn through life. The dream that our Father has dreamed for each was at the forefront of His thoughts when He lovingly and purposefully wove us together in our mother's womb. There, with our personal destiny in mind as His driving force, He made us with everything we would need to fulfill it. Our confidence is that the circumstances of life will bring our destiny to the forefront of fulfillment so that our contribution to the planet may be made to its fullest intention. This is our peace and, most certainly, this is our rest. Unfortunately, however, many believers are as disconnected from their King as everyone else in the world. Few of us have come to understand that our faith is far more than a confession. Rather, our faith is rooted in experience born of actual interaction with the Divine. This conscious interaction keeps us connected both to Him and to reality—life as it really is (*I Am a Son*, 121).

Further Evidence

> *You watched me as I was being formed in utter seclusion, as I was woven together in the dark of the womb. You saw me before I was born. Every day of my life was recorded in your book. Every moment was laid out before a single day had passed* (Psalm 139:15-16).

> *And we know that God causes everything to work together for the good of those who love God and are called according to his purpose for them* (Romans 8:28).

> *And let the peace that comes from Christ rule in your hearts. For as members of one body you are called to live in peace. And always be thankful* (Colossians 3:15).

REFLECT: SEEING THE INVISIBLE

(Remember to circle, underline, or otherwise highlight any words or images that stand out to you in the devotional or the related Scriptures. Include them in your journaling response.)

You are not here by accident. God made you on purpose with a purpose in mind. All that you do flows from that purpose. Take time in the Presence of Jesus to reflect on the themes that flow from you naturally—the gifts and abilities God invested in you when He created you in your mother's womb.

RESPOND

Journal your response about the gifts and abilities God has invested in your life here.

How will I make this visible through my life today?

....

....

....

....

....

....

....

....

....

....

....

....

....

....

....

....

....

....

65

WE ARE ALL ON A JOURNEY INTO THE VERY HEART OF GOD

READ

We are on a journey. It is a journey that leads us directly into the King where there is new light, possibilities, and new hope. The scenery of that journey naturally changes as we go forward. Indeed, if there is no change of scenery, there is no movement. When there is no movement, there is no real journey. We thought we were looking for a city made without hands, whose builder and maker is God. We soon discovered that that city is us wherein are the streets of God, where there is no darkness, where the King dwells in plain sight to all who can truly see. Now we know that He alone is the quest, the prize whose ultimate union results in purpose and destiny now, in this life. Now, ours is a journey to discover the wonders of this Divine union right now. It is a journey that requires a depth of brokenness that covets personal instruction and clarification of everything that will enhance union with Him. It is hungry enough, desperate enough for the sovereign rule of the King within to make any adjustments necessary to see His reign established within (*Forgotten Mountain*, 23).

Further Evidence

> *For God wanted them to know that the riches and glory of Christ are for you Gentiles, too. And this is the secret: Christ lives in you. This gives you assurance of sharing his glory* (Colossians 1:27).

> *Forgetting the past and looking forward to what lies ahead, I press on to reach the end of the race and receive the heavenly prize for which God, through Christ Jesus, is calling us* (Philippians 3:13-14).

> *And may you have the power to understand, as all God's people should, how wide, how long, how high, and how deep his love is. May you experience the love of Christ, though it is too great to understand fully. Then you will be made complete with all the fullness of life and power that comes from God* (Ephesians 3:18-19).

REFLECT: SEEING THE INVISIBLE

(Remember to circle, underline, or otherwise highlight any words or images that stand out to you in the devotional or the related Scriptures. Include them in your journaling response.)

All journeys are made one step at a time, including your own spiritual journey. Take some time in the Presence of Jesus to reflect on your own journey into greater devotion to Him.

RESPOND

Journal about your spiritual journey of devotion to Jesus here.

How will I make this visible through my life today?

66

THE NEARNESS OF THE KING BRINGS NEW ORDER TO OUR LIVES

READ

When the King is near—rather, when the King rules—things are put back into Divine order, His order. The King expresses Himself in ways that require heart change before any real external change can be accomplished. Yes, when the King truly reigns, things change. Everything is turned upside down. Systems are broken down; authority is redefined; the land is healed; and prosperity is restored in body, soul, and spirit. In short, everything is transformed. The first become last and the last, first. Leaders become servants and servants become leaders. To live, one understands he must first die. To be truly wealthy, it becomes clear that you must first give away all you have. Life becomes noble, fulfilling, hopeful, refreshing, full of peace and inner contentment. The journey is simplified (*Forgotten Mountain*, 27).

Further Evidence

But as for me, how good it is to be near God! I have made the Sovereign Lord my shelter, and will tell everyone about the wonderful things you do (Psalm 73:28).

Now it will come about that in the last days the mountain of the house of the Lord will be established as the chief of the mountains, and will be raised above the hills; and all the nations will stream to it (Isaiah 2:2 NASB).

So those who are last now will be first then, and those who are first will be last (Matthew 20:16).

REFLECT: SEEING THE INVISIBLE

(Remember to circle, underline, or otherwise highlight any words or images that stand out to you in the devotional or the related Scriptures. Include them in your journaling response.)

God builds everything the same way from the inside out. It is no different with His order in you. He might turn your life inside out here and there. He is focused on your heart.

RESPOND

Journal here about some of the ways God is changing your priorities and reordering your life along the way of your journey.

How will I make this visible through my life.

67

OUR DESTINY IS TRUE INNER, CONTAGIOUS PEACE

READ

Blessed are the peacemakers. The world is desperate for someone, anyone who can bring true godly peace and harmony to the world. The King told us, *"Peace I leave with you; My peace I give to you; not as the world gives do I give to you"* (John 14:27 NASB). The peace that the King gives is not just absence of armed conflict. His peace is not the suppression of anger, ignoring animosity, or redefining hate. His peace is an authentic state of being as a result of inner contentment. His peace does not react in anger, does not look for revenge, and is seldom offended. His peace envelopes the whole person, body, soul, and spirit, until they naturally become an agent of peace. Yes, there are peacemakers—those who have done far more than study the course. They have given of themselves for a cause much greater than their own or any earthly institution or human cause. They daily give themselves for a peace that is otherworldly in origin but very present in its expression in time and space (*Forgotten Mountain*, 49).

Further Evidence

> *You will keep in perfect peace all who trust in you, all whose thoughts are fixed on you!* (Isaiah 26:3)

> *I am leaving you with a gift—peace of mind and heart. And the peace I give is a gift the world cannot give. So don't be troubled or afraid* (John 14:27).

> *Not that I was ever in need, for I have learned how to be content with whatever I have* (Philippians 4:11).

> *Now may the Lord of peace himself give you his peace at all times and in every situation. The Lord be with you all* (2 Thessalonians 3:16).

REFLECT: SEEING THE INVISIBLE

(Remember to circle, underline, or otherwise highlight any words or images that stand out to you in the devotional or the related Scriptures. Include them in your journaling response.)

You long to just take a deep breath sometimes—a space filled with peace and contentment where you can see and think clearly. Many of us lack the true peace that flows from the inside out. Peace is a heart condition. When we are at peace we change the atmosphere around us.

RESPOND

Take time in the Presence of Jesus to receive that peace. Journal your response here.

How will I make this visible through my life today?

....

....

....

....

....

....

....

....

....

....

....

....

....

....

....

....

....

....

68

AS SUBJECTS OF THE KING WE ARE AMBASSADORS FOR HIS KINGDOM

READ

These emerging peacemakers are true ambassadors and have submitted themselves to the King. They have offered themselves, their hearts, their wills, their futures to the work of the King. They have voluntarily given their lives that He might set up His Kingdom, the government within their hearts. These have seen and understood that the hope of the world is not in the failed political theory of past governments and religions. There must, most certainly, be genuine inner governance of the individual heart. The future, if it is to be the shining beacon of hope that most want it to be, will be formed by the King who has set up His Kingdom within and rules the hearts of those who not only believe in Him and in His words but actually believe Him to the point that they surrender their hearts to His Kingdom rule within, the inner governance of the heart (*Forgotten Mountain*, 50).

Further Evidence

Arise, Jerusalem! Let your light shine for all to see. For the glory of the Lord rises to shine on you. Darkness as black as night covers all the nations of the earth, but the glory of the Lord rises and appears over you. All nations will come to your light; mighty kings will come to see your radiance (Isaiah 60:1-3).

One day the Pharisees asked Jesus, "When will the Kingdom of God come?" Jesus replied, "The Kingdom of God can't be detected by visible signs. You won't be able to say, 'Here it is!' or 'It's over there!' For the Kingdom of God is already among you" (Luke 17:20-21).

So we are Christ's ambassadors; God is making his appeal through us. We speak for Christ when we plead, "Come back to God!" (2 Corinthians 5:20)

REFLECT: SEEING THE INVISIBLE

(Remember to circle, underline, or otherwise highlight any words or images that stand out to you in the devotional or the related Scriptures. Include them in your journaling response.)

The Kingdom of God is more than signs; it is a condition of the heart—an inner government with you as its ambassador. How is this inner government expressed throughout your life? Sit in the Presence of Jesus and receive your ambassadorship.

RESPOND

Journal your response here about what it means to be an ambassador of Jesus and His Kingdom.

How will I make this visible through my life today?

69

GOD WILL LEAD YOU
TO YOUR DESTINY

READ

Don't be afraid of your uniqueness. You are who you are for the purpose that the King has designed. He knows what that is and He is committed to see you thrive in that purpose. It is His commitment to you, His dream. It is His moment-by-moment guidance that will bring it about. Your moment-by-moment surrender will insure that it unfolds in its fullness with an immeasurable impact in this life and in the spirit. One thing is perfectly clear once you have seen the King. All life matters. More to the point, all life is essential, for if you are here, God has ordained it. If God ordained it, it has purpose. If you breathe, you have the potential within you to function, flourish, thrive as an ambassador of the King (*Forgotten Mountain*, 57).

Further Evidence

> *The Lord directs the steps of the godly. He delights in every detail of their lives* (Psalm 37:23).

Thank you for making me so wonderfully complex! Your workmanship is marvelous—how well I know it (Psalm 139:14).

Since God chose you to be the holy people he loves, you must clothe yourselves with tenderhearted mercy, kindness, humility, gentleness, and patience (Colossians 3:12).

REFLECT: SEEING THE INVISIBLE

(Remember to circle, underline, or otherwise highlight any words or images that stand out to you in the devotional or the related Scriptures. Include them in your journaling response.)

Your purpose is as unique as your fingerprints. There are no copies of you. Take time in the Presence of Jesus to reflect on your own uniqueness and life experiences and how God has redeemed them for Himself.

RESPOND

Journal here about how your life experiences have prepared you for God's purposes. How might God redeem and repurpose those experiences?

How will I make this visible through my life today?

70

OUR PURPOSE IS TO CARRY THE LIFE OF THE KING

READ

When the King is allowed to set up His life within, there is a transformational union between the King and man. We now call him the God-man. He is neither under the slavery of his instinctive animal nature nor is he condescending to those of a religious belief system. Something very powerful happens. Something otherworldly blossoms within man. He no longer lives for himself, but he lives for the well-being of all men. He does not condemn; he saves. He does not build walls of separation; he gathers. He does not silence or discredit the opposing voice; he listens. He may disagree, but he loves and empowers them. He allows the King to live and love through him. The attributes, power, and purposes of the King's life are of paramount importance to these God-men, and to that end they live and to that end they sometimes die (*Forgotten Mountain*, 60).

Further Evidence

> *He died for everyone so that those who receive his new life will no longer live for themselves. Instead, they will live for Christ, who died and was raised for them* (2 Corinthians 5:15).

> *And so, dear brothers and sisters, I plead with you to give your bodies to God because of all he has done for you. Let them be a living and holy sacrifice—the kind he will find acceptable* (Romans 12:1).

> *My old self has been crucified with Christ. It is no longer I who live, but Christ lives in me. So I live in this earthly body by trusting in the Son of God, who loved me and gave himself for me* (Galatians 2:20).

REFLECT: SEEING THE INVISIBLE

(Remember to circle, underline, or otherwise highlight any words or images that stand out to you in the devotional or the related Scriptures. Include them in your journaling response.)

Your life as a child of God is grounded in trust. Who do you trust? As you sit with Jesus, invite Him to tell you of areas in your heart He wants you to grow in trusting Him.

RESPOND

Journal about those areas of growing trust in your heart. How will I make this visible through my life today?

71

THE KINGDOM OF GOD INCREASES IN US WITH OUR SURRENDER

READ

Authentic transformation is the supernatural activity of the King in the heart of an individual. The heart changes, is transformed when there is clear, absolute surrender in an area of one's life. This surrender, also called repentance, releases the power and purposes of God to replace the surrendered area with the life of Christ, the King of the mountain of the Lord. As Paul the apostle confessed, "*I die daily*" (1 Cor. 15:31 NASB). Death to the earthy side of us releases the spiritual force of God to gain access to our mind, thus changing it to represent the new thing that is now happening within our hearts. The more sincere the surrender, the more radical the takeover of the King within. No wonder those who are forgiven rejoice much. Surrender releases the burden of regret, shame, guilt, and inner torment that reigns when our fleshy self-controls our lives. There is no doubt that the rule of the

King produces peace where there was once only the pain of failure (*Forgotten Mountain*, 77).

Further Evidence

> *Come to Me, all who are weary and heavy-laden, and I will give you rest. Take My yoke upon you and learn from Me, for I am gentle and humble in heart, and you will find rest for your souls. For My yoke is easy and My burden is light* (Matthew 11:28-30 NASB).

> *Then he said to the crowd, "If any of you wants to be my follower, you must give up your own way, take up your cross daily, and follow me"* (Luke 9:23).

> *Therefore, since we are surrounded by such a huge crowd of witnesses to the life of faith, let us strip off every weight that slows us down, especially the sin that so easily trips us up. And let us run with endurance the race God has set before us* (Hebrews 12:1).

REFLECT: SEEING THE INVISIBLE

(Remember to circle, underline, or otherwise highlight any words or images that stand out to you in the devotional or the related Scriptures. Include them in your journaling response.)

Your surrender to the King is a decision to follow the heart and footsteps of Jesus rather than your own. Surrender to the King means more freedom, not less. Sit quietly with Jesus and surrender your next steps to Him.

RESPOND

Journal here about the next steps to be surrendered to Jesus.
How will I make this visible through my life today?

....

....

....

....

....

....

....

....

....

....

....

....

....

....

....

....

....

....

....

72

THE KING'S REIGN OVERSHADOWS OUR LIVES

READ

As men and women become more aware of His life within them, they are more acutely aware that man's ways are clearly not the ways of his Lord. His own ego becomes a glaring obstacle to the ways of his King who dwells within him. These emerging kings become appalled at the rise of their own fleshy retorts and humanistic gerrymandering for the expediency of a particular group. He is finding that he cannot stray from the heart of the King, for his heart has been renewed with the heart of the King. The demands of his selfish heart are now the enemy of his deepest desires. He will never execute a policy under the guise of spiritual correctness when it clearly does not resonate with the purposes of the King whom he claims to represent. The King is not looking for folks to act like Him. He is in search of those who will die to their egotistical pride, selfish ambition, and personal kingdoms to be part of something much bigger than they that is eternal, peaceful, compassionate, and authentic to the deepest part of their hearts (*Forgotten Mountain*, 87-88).

Further Evidence

> *Then I will sprinkle clean water on you, and you will be clean. Your filth will be washed away, and you will no longer worship idols. And I will give you a new heart, and I will put a new spirit in you. I will take out your stony, stubborn heart and give you a tender, responsive heart* (Ezekiel 36:25-26).

> *Because you are my helper, I sing for joy in the shadow of your wings* (Psalm 63:7).

> *He must increase, but I must decrease* (John 3:30 NASB).

> *This means that anyone who belongs to Christ has become a new person. The old life is gone; a new life has begun!* (2 Corinthians 5:17)

REFLECT: SEEING THE INVISIBLE

(Remember to circle, underline, or otherwise highlight any words or images that stand out to you in the devotional or the related Scriptures. Include them in your journaling response.)

In order to be filled, a vessel must first be emptied. Take time in this present moment to pour out the distractions of the day and allow Jesus to fill you.

RESPOND

Write your response here concerning the life of Jesus being poured into you.

How will I make this visible through my life today?

....

....

....

....

....

....

....

....

....

....

....

....

....

....

....

....

....

....

....

73

YOU ARE CALLED INTO A PRIESTHOOD OF GOD'S PRESENCE

READ

From the beginning until the end, the purpose of God for man was singular. He wants a priesthood through whom He can love the world as only He can in kindness, mercy, peace, and wholeness. It is not in the nature of man to put others first, to seek the good of all in spite of the obstacles, to be the servant, the giver. Maybe that is why our King saw fit to rule through the likes of difficult and resistive folks like me. We must voluntarily, consciously, and decisively reject our self-centered, self-preserving nature to allow the King to do what no man can in himself. We have the possibility at our disposal to be the priests of Melchizedek, the throne of the King, the Lamp of the Anointed, the city on a hill, the Voice of the Beloved, the portal through whom the world may gaze on the wondrous King. He is calling mere mortal man to be transformed into the image and very likeness of the King, who *is* the mountain of the house of the Lord (*Forgotten Mountain*, 102).

Further Evidence

> *"And you shall be to Me a kingdom of priests and a holy nation." These are the words that you shall speak to the sons of Israel* (Exodus 19:6 NASB).

> *And you are living stones that God is building into his spiritual temple. What's more, you are his holy priests. Through the mediation of Jesus Christ, you offer spiritual sacrifices that please God* (1 Peter 2:5).

> *And they sang a new song saying: "You are worthy to take the scroll, and to open its seals; for You were slain, and have redeemed us to God by Your blood out of every tribe and tongue and people and nation, and have made us kings and priests to our God; and we shall reign on the earth"* (Revelation 5:9-10 NKJV).

REFLECT: SEEING THE INVISIBLE

(Remember to circle, underline, or otherwise highlight any words or images that stand out to you in the devotional or the related Scriptures. Include them in your journaling response.)

You are called to offer the spiritual sacrifices of prayer and intercession. You are called to life beyond yourself. What do you find yourself praying about in the Presence of God? As you quiet yourself in the Presence of Jesus, allow Him to shape your prayer.

RESPOND

Journal about what you and Jesus are praying together.
How will I make this visible through my life today?

74

YOU HAVE ACCESS TO THE PRESENCE OF GOD THROUGH THE BLOOD OF CHRIST

READ

When God sent the King to the earth, He sent the King to redeem mankind so the law would be fulfilled. In short, He gave all men the possibility to be priests to God. He forgave their sin, cleansed them from their penchant toward sin, filled them with the Presence of the King for the purpose of changing the heart of man so that they would, by nature, surrender themselves to God. Because of what the King accomplished on the earth, all men could now not only approach God but have fellowship with Him. Not because man was perfect but because he was redeemed from the consequences of the law. Now man could approach God with confidence knowing that the blood of the King covered man's imperfection until the power and love of the King was able to change him. By presenting themselves to the King for inner transformation and governance, man would be empowered and changed by the very Presence of the King within (*Forgotten Mountain*, 106).

Further Evidence

> *With your unfailing love you lead the people you have redeemed. In your might, you guide them to your sacred home* (Exodus 15:13).

> *Then they remembered that God was their rock, that God Most High was their redeemer* (Psalm 78:35).

> *This is what the Lord says—your Redeemer, the Holy One of Israel: "I am the Lord your God, who teaches you what is good for you and leads you along the paths you should follow"* (Isaiah 48:17).

> *So let us come boldly to the throne of our gracious God. There we will receive his mercy, and we will find grace to help us when we need it most* (Hebrews 4:16).

REFLECT: SEEING THE INVISIBLE

(Remember to circle, underline, or otherwise highlight any words or images that stand out to you in the devotional or the related Scriptures. Include them in your journaling response.)

It is an awesome thought that you might enter into the very Presence of God, yet even more powerful that His Presence enters you. That Presence fills you and flows from you. Settle yourself in the Presence of God and be filled with awe resulting in worship.

RESPOND

Try your hand at writing a psalm of praise to the Lord as you enter His Presence and as His Presence enters you.

How will I make this visible through my life today?

....

....

....

....

....

....

....

....

....

....

....

....

....

....

....

....

....

....

75

SONS AND DAUGHTERS OF GOD PRODUCE THE FRUIT OF HIS KINGDOM

READ

God's big idea was to extend His kingly influence and culture from the celestial to the terrestrial by planting Garden communities throughout the earth that would perfectly reflect the richness and abundant life of His heavenly Kingdom. And He chose to do it through citizen-servants like you and me who will seek first His Kingdom and His righteousness and live exclusively for Him. We do this by humbling ourselves and giving ourselves freely to others so that they may see Him in us, learn of His Kingdom from us, and apply for citizenship themselves. Let us be faithful to our calling and hasten the day when *"the earth will be filled with the knowledge of the glory of the Lord as the waters cover the sea"* (Hab. 2:14 NIV) (*Forgotten Mountain*, 175).

Further Evidence

For as the waters fill the sea, the earth will be filled with an awareness of the glory of the Lord (Habakkuk 2:14).

No, O people, the Lord has told you what is good, and this is what he requires of you: to do what is right, to love mercy, and to walk humbly with your God (Micah 6:8).

Seek the Kingdom of God above all else, and live righteously, and he will give you everything you need (Matthew 6:33).

Since God chose you to be the holy people he loves, you must clothe yourselves with tenderhearted mercy, kindness, humility, gentleness, and patience (Colossians 3:12).

REFLECT: SEEING THE INVISIBLE

(Remember to circle, underline, or otherwise highlight any words or images that stand out to you in the devotional or the related Scriptures. Include them in your journaling response.)

True humility is getting out the way so that the world can see God. The basis of your humility is knowing that you are subjects of the King.

RESPOND

Journal here about how you see yourself as a subject of the King.

How will I make this visible through my life today?

76

THE KING IS COMING...
WITHIN YOU!

READ

We are only visiting this planet. We are sojourning in this land of time and space and flesh and blood. His Kingdom is coming. The permanent restoration of the King's Presence in the earth, in us, in me is the hope we long for. It is the solution we have believed for. It brings rest to the weary heart and health to those who love Him with love undying. He carries true destiny into the hearts of His own and fulfillment to all who have hoped in His appearing. We will build no monuments, no towers. We will keep our hearts open and our spirits unfurled like a sail of ship, waiting for the wind of God to take us to our next adventure. For the wind blows where it will. We hear the sound of it, but we do not know where it has come from or where it is going. So is everyone who is born of His Spirit. But our bags are packed and we are ready to respond to His voice, wherever He may lead. This is the secret of moving on with God (*Secrets of the Most Holy Place*, 99-10).

Further Evidence

"Look! I am sending my messenger, and he will prepare the way before me. Then the Lord you are seeking will suddenly come to his Temple. The messenger of the covenant, whom you look for so eagerly, is surely coming," says the Lord of Heaven's Armies (Malachi 3:1).

Suddenly, the angel was joined by a vast host of others— the armies of heaven—praising God and saying, "Glory to God in highest heaven, and peace on earth to those with whom God is pleased" (Luke 2:13-14).

For all who are led by the Spirit of God are children of God (Romans 8:14).

REFLECT: SEEING THE INVISIBLE

(Remember to circle, underline, or otherwise highlight any words or images that stand out to you in the devotional or the related Scriptures. Include them in your journaling response.)

The King is coming moment by moment to claim His throne in your heart. Is there anything or anyone else occupying that throne? Sit quietly with the King and invite Him to take His rightful place.

RESPOND

Envision your heart as a throne and journal here concerning anything or anyone who might be enthroned there other than Jesus.

How will I make this visible through my life today?

77

WE HAVE BEEN ENTRUSTED WITH THE GLORY OF GOD

READ

The ultimate goal in my sojourn through this life is not to make it easy on myself. My goal is to make it so that my Father can trust me and use me. I want the world to see Him through my actions, whether or not I ever open my mouth. My passion is to be as close to an exact representation of His Kingdom as I possibly can. Authenticity is the only thing that will cause the nations to run to Him. The world looks at Christianity in general and sees nothing that causes them to run to our light. Most believers blame the devil and anything else that comes to mind as to why this is so. There is something grossly missing in our faith experience, our faith expression, and our belief system when the nations run away from us rather than to us (*I Am a Son*, 113).

Further Evidence

> *Then the Lord came down in a cloud and stood there with him; and he called out his own name, Yahweh. The*

Lord passed in front of Moses, calling out, "Yahweh! The Lord! The God of compassion and mercy! I am slow to anger and filled with unfailing love and faithfulness" (Exodus 34:5-6).

Then the glory of the Lord will be revealed, and all people will see it together. The Lord has spoken! (Isaiah 40:5)

So we are Christ's ambassadors; God is making his appeal through us. We speak for Christ when we plead, "Come back to God!" (2 Corinthians 5:20)

REFLECT: SEEING THE INVISIBLE

(Remember to circle, underline, or otherwise highlight any words or images that stand out to you in the devotional or the related Scriptures. Include them in your journaling response.)

The glory of a person is what makes them unique above all others. God is no exception. He is compassionate, gracious, slow to anger, above all filled with mercy and faithfulness. You carry the very glory of God into the world around you. Consider the words of Exodus 34:5-6 above.

RESPOND

Take time to reflect on these words in your journaling; describe the very glory of God. How does your life express these words?

How will I make this visible though my life today?

78

GOD'S ULTIMATE INTENTION IS THAT WE WOULD BE ONE WITH HIM

READ

[God's] ultimate intention is to have those who will allow Him to establish His governance within their hearts. This King wanted more than I understood. He wanted me. He wanted to use me as His beachhead in establishing His Kingdom on this planet. I would see wonders beyond my imagination, and I would experience a fellowship with the King that others only dream about. The best I had going for me was that the yearning of my heart was out of my control. My heart ached for Him, for His life, His love within. But this King does not show favorites. He moves on us all equally, drawing us all to His inner dwelling place, our hearts, where we experience true union with the Divine (*Forgotten Mountain*, 36).

Further Evidence

I pray that they will all be one, just as you and I are one—as you are in me, Father, and I am in you. And may they be in us so that the world will believe you sent me (John 17:21).

But the person who is joined to the Lord is one spirit with him (1 Corinthians 6:17).

Some of us are Jews, some are Gentiles, some are slaves, and some are free. But we have all been baptized into one body by one Spirit, and we all share the same Spirit (1 Corinthians 12:13).

REFLECT: SEEING THE INVISIBLE

(Remember to circle, underline, or otherwise highlight any words or images that stand out to you in the devotional or the related Scriptures. Include them in your journaling response.)

As you come to know God more deeply, your love becomes longing. This longing leads you to want to spend your attention on the One who loves you deeply. Give yourself to that longing as you spend time with Jesus.

RESPOND

Journal about your love for God the Father, Son, and Spirit. How will I make this visible through my life today?

79

WE SHARE IN JESUS' VICTORY OVER SIN, DEATH, AND THE ENEMIES OF THE KINGDOM OF GOD

READ

Man needs more than a list of the right things to do; he needs a King. He needs a King who will reign righteously, love unconditionally, rule with justice and equity. This is the King who has every intention to reign first within the heart of man. The King understands that the only hope of success that man has is to be ruled by One who has already conquered death, human passion, and the enemy himself. Let us not forget that the King faced the enemies of His soul and He won. He overcame. He destroyed the power of His enemy and ours. It is fitting, then, that the conquering King take up residence within, establishing His victorious Kingdom in our hearts as well. He has already won the war, not just a battle. Surrendering to the One who is victorious, aligning our hearts to His, makes His victory ours (*Forgotten Mountain*, 39).

Further Evidence

Be still, and know that I am God! I will be honored by every nation. I will be honored throughout the world (Psalm 46:10).

I am leaving you with a gift—peace of mind and heart. And the peace I give is a gift the world cannot give. So don't be troubled or afraid (John 14:27).

I have told you all this so that you may have peace in me. Here on earth you will have many trials and sorrows. But take heart, because I have overcome the world (John 16:33).

And the result of God's gracious gift is very different from the result of that one man's sin. For Adam's sin led to condemnation, but God's free gift leads to our being made right with God, even though we are guilty of many sins (Romans 5:16).

REFLECT: SEEING THE INVISIBLE

(Remember to circle, underline, or otherwise highlight any words or images that stand out to you in the devotional or the related Scriptures. Include them in your journaling response.)

Sometimes you struggle to gain a victory that Jesus has already won. What are you fighting with? Accept the free gift of God's grace based on the victory Jesus has already won for you.

RESPOND

Take time to journal in the Presence of Jesus, expressing thanks for His gift to you.

How will I make this visible through my life today?

80

When God Changes Us, We Change Everything Around Us

Read

Once [God's] heart of love and compassion is seen and understood, anything contrary to Him is easily identified and rejected. Our King is not interested in the seats of secular government; He is passionate about the seat of man's heart. His plan is, as it has always been, to win the man. When the heart of man is won, everything around him changes. If someone is in government then the government changes. If the person is in business then the business changes; if in education, education changes; if entertainment, then entertainment changes, and so on. When man fails to experience a heart change, laws are enacted to force people into an attitude of obedience (*Forgotten Mountain*, 93).

Further Evidence

> *You are the light of the world—like a city on a hilltop that cannot be hidden* (Matthew 5:14).

> *You are the salt of the earth. But what good is salt if it has lost its flavor? Can you make it salty again? It will be thrown out and trampled underfoot as worthless* (Matthew 5:13).

> *However, he has given each one of us a special gift through the generosity of Christ* (Ephesians 4:7).

REFLECT: SEEING THE INVISIBLE

(Remember to circle, underline, or otherwise highlight any words or images that stand out to you in the devotional or the related Scriptures. Include them in your journaling response.)

The early Christians turned the world around them upside down (see Acts 17:6). The Presence of God through your life changes everything around you as well. Think about your own sphere of influence—whether in your profession or the arts or another realm. Reflect on how you may bring the influence of the life of Jesus within you to your world.

RESPOND

Journal about Jesus bringing His influence into your world through your life.

How will I make this visible through my life today?

81

JESUS ABANDONED HIS THRONE FOR THOSE WHO ABANDON THEMSELVES TO HIM

READ

[God's] ultimate intention [is] the gathering of all men to Himself. His passionate love is single-minded, acutely focused on bringing all men to the reign of the King within, thus bringing true and tangible peace the earth in the daily experience of wonder and peace of His Kingdom. Yes, it can clearly be said it is God who is gathering to Himself those who will come, those who will say "yes." He is putting into our hearts an indefinable and unexplainable devotion to Him. He is blowing the wind of His Spirit into the hearts of those who have abandoned themselves to Him with utmost trust, having raised the sail of their spirit into the wind of God, which will ever blow us into Himself (*Forgotten Mountain*, 138; *Secrets of the Most Holy Place*, 75).

Further Evidence

He [Solomon] *prayed, "O Lord, God of Israel, there is no God like you in all of heaven and earth. You keep your covenant and show unfailing love to all who walk before you in wholehearted devotion"* (2 Chronicles 6:14).

The wind blows wherever it wants. Just as you can hear the wind but can't tell where it comes from or where it is going, so you can't explain how people are born of the Spirit (John 3:8).

You must have the same attitude that Christ Jesus had. Though he was God, he did not think of equality with God as something to cling to. Instead, he gave up his divine privileges he took the humble position of a slave and was born as a human being (Philippians 2:5-7).

REFLECT: SEEING THE INVISIBLE

(Remember to circle, underline, or otherwise highlight any words or images that stand out to you in the devotional or the related Scriptures. Include them in your journaling response.)

The Son of God left His throne behind to rescue you from yourself. That is the essence of love. How does this make you feel about yourself? What kind of self-talk comes up in your mind when you consider the great rescue of Jesus?

RESPOND

Take time to journal your reflections here. Allow Jesus to speak the truth of His love for you.

How will I make this visible through my life today?

82

JESUS PRAYED THAT WE WOULD LOOK JUST LIKE HIM—LIKE HIS FATHER

READ

The life of Jesus was and is the very image of who our Father is. We all love to quote the scripture, "I only do what I see my Father in heaven doing" (see John 5:19), but I doubt that we understand its implications. Many have referenced this verse when teaching about miracles. However, there is a far more important aspect to what Jesus said here. Let's put that verse together with these: "*I and My Father are one*" (John 10:30 NKJV), and again, "*He who has seen Me has seen the Father*" (John 14:9 NKJV). Nothing could be clearer concerning the desire of our Elder Brother toward His Father. He wanted the world to see the compassionate, loving, forgiving, gentle Father as He truly is. He wanted humanity to know the gracious, gathering, healing heart of His Father the way He already knew Him. Jesus knew that the world, who could not see His Father would judge His Father by the actions, attitudes, and lifestyle of His Son *(I am a Son*, 154).

Further Evidence

> *The Father and I are one* (John 10:30).

> *Jesus replied, "Have I been with you all this time, Philip, and yet you still don't know who I am? Anyone who has seen me has seen the Father! So why are you asking me to show him to you?"* (John 14:9)

> *The Son radiates God's own glory and expresses the very character of God, and he sustains everything by the mighty power of his command. When he had cleansed us from our sins, he sat down in the place of honor at the right hand of the majestic God in heaven* (Hebrews 1:3).

REFLECT: SEEING THE INVISIBLE

(Remember to circle, underline, or otherwise highlight any words or images that stand out to you in the devotional or the related Scriptures. Include them in your journaling response.)

Your life in Christ gives the world insight into Jesus. Jesus looked exactly like the Father. He had the same character of love and compassion demonstrated in the life of humility. Live a life focused on the face of Jesus until we look like Him.

RESPOND

Sit in the Presence of Jesus and journal your answer. Who do you look like?

How will I make this visible through my life today?

....

....

....

....

....

....

....

....

....

....

....

....

....

....

....

....

....

....

83

OBEDIENCE IS THE WAY INTO THE PURPOSE GOD

READ

If you want the joy of the Lord to return to you, if you want His Presence and power to return to your spirit, if you are wondering why you are not being renewed—yield to the very thing God is saying to you. Obedience brings the joy of the Lord, peace, and fulfillment. Your unabashed yieldedness will cause God's next dream for you to begin to happen in another dimension, in a higher place, preparing for it to break through time and space, directly into your life. He takes you to a supernatural place. I can see it right now in my spirit; eternity is always breaking through time and space. He hears your prayers. You are forgiven, guilt-free. He is after you. He is chasing you down. He is saying you are going to learn how deep and wide His love is (*God Out of Control*, 27-28).

Further Evidence

> *The heavens proclaim the glory of God. The skies display his craftsmanship. Day after day they continue to speak;*

night after night they make him known. They speak without a sound or word; their voice is never heard. Yet their message has gone throughout the earth, and their words to all the world (Psalm 19:1-4).

Then he said to the crowd, "If any of you wants to be my follower, you must give up your own way, take up your cross daily, and follow me" (Luke 9:23).

Dear friends, if we don't feel guilty, we can come to God with bold confidence. And we will receive from him whatever we ask because we obey him and do the things that please him (1 John 3:21-22).

REFLECT: SEEING THE INVISIBLE

(Remember to circle, underline, or otherwise highlight any words or images that stand out to you in the devotional or the related Scriptures. Include them in your journaling response.)

God is speaking to you all the time by the Spirit through your spirit. Obedience is the proof that you are hearing Him. Are there things God is speaking through your circumstances, other people, or in the intimacy of your spirit that you have not stepped into?

RESPOND

Sit with Jesus and write about your first steps to fulfilling His purpose through you.

How will I make this visible through my life today?

84

NOTHING CAN SEPARATE US FROM THE LOVE OF GOD!

READ

God knows your frailty, and He knows your weaknesses. Don't let guilt rob you of your destiny. Guilt robs you if you allow it. You may be thinking, *But I screwed up lots of times, and I don't allow God to control my life, and I told God "no" lots of times.* Nonetheless, the purposes of God are sure, and His plan for you is secure and eternal. All you have to do is turn back to the Lord and say, "Lord, I failed, but I know You forgive me in Jesus' name." Don't let guilt of the past keep you from your destiny. *Sin does not disqualify us.* Yes, it is true that we have sinned, but that sin does not disqualify us from His glory. Our sin does not separate us from His Presence. His blood is greater than our sin. His glory is greater than our sin. Forgiveness is greater than our sin. It is impossible to imagine a sin committed by a hungry believer that could separate him from the Lord who gave Himself on our behalf. Our sin cannot be stronger than His blood (*God Out of Control*, 28; *Secrets of the Most Holy Place*, 76).

Further Evidence

> *"Come now, let's settle this," says the Lord. "Though your sins are like scarlet, I will make them as white as snow. Though they are red like crimson, I will make them as white as wool"* (Isaiah 1:18).

> *And I am convinced that nothing can ever separate us from God's love. Neither death nor life, neither angels nor demons, neither our fears for today nor our worries about tomorrow—not even the powers of hell can separate us from God's love. No power in the sky above or in the earth below—indeed, nothing in all creation will ever be able to separate us from the love of God that is revealed in Christ Jesus our Lord* (Romans 8:38-39).

REFLECT: SEEING THE INVISIBLE

(Remember to circle, underline, or otherwise highlight any words or images that stand out to you in the devotional or the related Scriptures. Include them in your journaling response.)

On your journey into the heart and purposes of God, you sometimes try to hide your flaws and imperfections. Nothing is invisible to God. He sees you every step of your journey and continues to call you to Himself. Listen to His invitation to you: "Come!"

RESPOND

Journal your response to the invitation of Jesus.
How will I make this visible through my life today?

85

The King Is Coming to His Sanctuary—Our Hearts

Read

God has never intended His Church to be without a King. He has never intended the throne room of the holy of holies (our hearts) to be unoccupied. His intention from the very beginning was for the King to dwell there, to have His throne in the midst of His people. Now one thing we know for certain is that He *will have* a people who will allow Him to dwell within them. That people might be small or great in number; they may appear to be light years ahead of everybody else. But they are people who are satisfied with nothing less than God's abiding Presence. They will not give up; they are not quitters. They're not satisfied with anything less than all that God has for them (*Manifest Presence*, 55-56).

Further Evidence

"Look! I am sending my messenger, and he will prepare the way before me. Then the Lord you are seeking will

suddenly come to his Temple. The messenger of the cove-
nant, whom you look for so eagerly, is surely coming," says
the Lord of Heaven's Armies (Malachi 3:1).

The Lord will reign forever. He will be your God, O
Jerusalem, throughout the generations. Then the seventh
angel blew his trumpet, and there were loud voices shout-
ing in heaven: Praise the Lord! (Psalm 146:10)

The world has now become the Kingdom of our Lord
and of his Christ, and he will reign forever and ever
(Revelation 11:15).

REFLECT: SEEING THE INVISIBLE

(Remember to circle, underline, or otherwise highlight any
words or images that stand out to you in the devotional or the
related Scriptures. Include them in your journaling response.)

A throne is a seat of power and authority. Whoever occupies
the throne occupies our thoughts and determines our peace.
Whose words are you speaking over yourself? Yours? Jesus'?
What kind of self-talk occupies the throne in your heart? Are
they thoughts of peace or self-criticism? What else? Sit with
Jesus and listen to the self-talk coming from the throne room
of your own heart.

RESPOND

Write about your self-talk here. Consider whether you can
hear Jesus speaking those words to you.

How will I make this visible through my life today?

86

GOD WORKS THROUGH HEARTS THAT ARE WILLING TO CHANGE

READ

[God] will work through hearts that are open and soft in their response to Him. He'll work through hearts that are flexible. He will work through people who are willing to have their plans changed, who are willing to have their careers changed, who are willing to have their homes changed, who are willing to have anything changed for the sake of serving God. Those are the people in whom God will establish His throne. And those are the people in whom God *is establishing* His throne today (*Manifest Presence*, 56).

Further Evidence

> *Don't copy the behavior and customs of this world, but let God transform you into a new person by changing the way you think. Then you will learn to know God's will for you, which is good and pleasing and perfect* (Romans 12:2).

So all of us who have had that veil removed can see and reflect the glory of the Lord. And the Lord—who is the Spirit—makes us more and more like him as we are changed into his glorious image (2 Corinthians 3:18).

It was by faith that Abraham obeyed when God called him to leave home and go to another land that God would give him as his inheritance. He went without knowing where he was going. And even when he reached the land God promised him, he lived there by faith—for he was like a foreigner, living in tents (Hebrews 11:8-9).

REFLECT: SEEING THE INVISIBLE

(Remember to circle, underline, or otherwise highlight any words or images that stand out to you in the devotional or the related Scriptures. Include them in your journaling response.)

How are you with changes that occur in your life? You will grow and increase in the purposes of God to the degree you can trust Him through the many changes along the way of your journey. Take time in the Presence of Jesus to reflect on changes that have occurred in your life and how you responded to those changes.

RESPOND

Journal here about where you saw God's hand in those changes.

How will I make this visible through my life today?

87

GOD IS ALWAYS MOVING YET ALWAYS A FAITHFUL SHELTER

READ

There is a depth of relationship in fellowship with Him that only those who have a burning passion for Him will ever experience. He wants us to *run* after Him. He does not want us to be content or satisfied with what we have or what we've experienced. There is a place of shelter, a relationship, a reality of the spiritual Presence of God that is for our experience in this life that will only be attained as we yield to Him with all our heart, with all our soul, with all our mind, and with all our strength. We too easily forget there is a vastness and limitlessness that God has for us. It is His manifest Presence and it is there for all who will respond—and keep on responding—to God's call in their lives (*Manifest Presence*, 120).

Further Evidence

> *Those who live in the shelter of the Most High will find rest in the shadow of the Almighty* (Psalm 91:1).

Take me with you; come, let's run! The king has brought me into his bedroom. How happy we are for you, O king. We praise your love even more than wine. How right they are to adore you (Song of Solomon 1:4).

Don't you realize that in a race everyone runs, but only one person gets the prize? So run to win! (1 Corinthians 9:24)

Therefore, since we are surrounded by such a huge crowd of witnesses to the life of faith, let us strip off every weight that slows us down, especially the sin that so easily trips us up. And let us run with endurance the race God has set before us (Hebrews 12:1).

REFLECT: SEEING THE INVISIBLE

(Remember to circle, underline, or otherwise highlight any words or images that stand out to you in the devotional or the related Scriptures. Include them in your journaling response.)

Your journey with Jesus is not about how fast you can run but how well. There are weights that drag you down and interfere with your ability to reach the finish line. As you sit quietly with Jesus, reflect on these weights that keep you from the prize, which is Jesus.

RESPOND

Journal here about Jesus releasing you from those weights that hold you back in your journey.

How will I make this visible through my life today?

88

AS CHILDREN OF GOD WE ARE ORDINARILY EXTRAORDINARY

READ

Yes, I *am* a son. I *am* human and I *am* divine. Only tomorrow will witness what we will do with the living Christ within, as He is released through otherwise ordinary folks. But now, as far as it is up to me and as far as I can access His mighty grace, I walk with dogged determination, divine anticipation, and unwavering assurance that He who began a good work in me will complete it, regardless of how others have settled for far less. The good work He is doing is not merely keeping me for Heaven. It is not maintaining just an outward appearance of holy living. This work of God is nothing less than the 10 percent man yielding to the 10 percent God who indwells him so that the world may know through tangible, physical demonstration in time and space that my Father has sent His Son to redeem, establish, and expand His mighty rule and reign in the earth—my earth first and then all of creation (*I Am a Son*, 31).

Further Evidence

The eyes of the Lord search the whole earth in order to strengthen those whose hearts are fully committed to him (2 Chronicles 16:9).

You won't be able to say, "Here it is!" or "It's over there!" For the Kingdom of God is already among you (Luke 17:21).

And I am certain that God, who began the good work within you, will continue his work until it is finally finished on the day when Christ Jesus returns (Philippians 1:6).

REFLECT: SEEING THE INVISIBLE

(Remember to circle, underline, or otherwise highlight any words or images that stand out to you in the devotional or the related Scriptures. Include them in your journaling response.)

Wherever you are on your journey into the heart and purpose of God the Lord will walk with you the whole way. You have come some distance in your journey. Every step has led you closer to the heart of Jesus. Sit with Jesus and reflect on a few of the milestones along the way.

RESPOND

Record a few of these milestones in your journaling here. How will I make this visible through my life today?

89

IN UNION WITH JESUS, HIS PURPOSE BECOMES OUR PURPOSE

READ

When Jesus taught us to pray, "Thy Kingdom come, Thy will be done on *earth* as it is in heaven," He laid down the pattern of redemption's plan for all things spiritual and all things natural. Understanding this simple principle keeps our spiritual ears attentive to the Voice of God and keeps our feet firmly planted on the ground. Staying in union with God makes us those through whom He will bring His ultimate plan into fruition. A humble acknowledgement of our sonship keeps us ready to do the bidding of the King for the sake of all creation. For truly, our destiny is wrapped up in the destiny of all things, and all creation is waiting and groaning for this moment. Let the sons arise! (*I Am a Son*, 127)

Further Evidence

> *Yes, I am the vine; you are the branches. Those who remain in me, and I in them, will produce much fruit.*

For apart from me you can do nothing. Anyone who does not remain in me is thrown away like a useless branch and withers. Such branches are gathered into a pile to be burned. But if you remain in me and my words remain in you, you may ask for anything you want, and it will be granted! When you produce much fruit, you are my true disciples. This brings great glory to my Father (John 15:5-8).

For all creation is waiting eagerly for that future day when God will reveal who his children really are. Against its will, all creation was subjected to God's curse. But with eager hope, the creation looks forward to the day when it will join God's children in glorious freedom from death and decay. For we know that all creation has been groaning as in the pains of childbirth right up to the present time (Romans 8:19-22).

REFLECT: SEEING THE INVISIBLE

(Remember to circle, underline, or otherwise highlight any words or images that stand out to you in the devotional or the related Scriptures. Include them in your journaling response.)

The Kingdom of God is like the fruit Jesus talked about in John 15. It is the fruit born by you as you abide in Jesus Christ. To abide is to remain in or connected to the heart and Presence of Jesus. When we are disconnected from Jesus we cannot produce Kingdom fruit.

RESPOND

As you journal today, stay intentionally connected to Jesus and reflect on your intimate connection with Him.

How will I make this visible through my life today?

....

....

....

....

....

....

....

....

....

....

....

....

....

....

....

....

....

....

....

....

....

....

90

YOUR JOURNEY INTO THE HEART OF JESUS CONTINUES

READ

The book has come to an end, but the journey continues. Transformation is an exhilarating lifelong experience. I know that as long as I breathe, I will always discover deeper opportunities to surrender to His will and experience more of His eternal life right here on this planet. The world's claim on my life grows weaker with each surrender. Paradoxically, my hiddenness in Him becomes more visible with each passing day as He increases in influence, love, and power within me. By His grace I will yield to Him. The conclusion to all of this will be the authentic and permanent transformation of our inner man. The nations will run to our King when they see Him as He really is, through you and me (*I Am a Son*, 160).

Further Evidence

> *I pray that from his glorious, unlimited resources he will empower you with inner strength through his Spirit* (Ephesians 3:16).

For you died to this life, and your real life is hidden with Christ in God (Colossians 3:3).

For God wanted them to know that the riches and glory of Christ are for you Gentiles, too. And this is the secret: Christ lives in you. This gives you assurance of sharing his glory (Colossians 1:27).

REFLECT: SEEING THE INVISIBLE

(Remember to circle, underline, or otherwise highlight any words or images that stand out to you in the devotional or the related Scriptures. Include them in your journaling response.)

Your journey continues until you see the face of Jesus and until the world sees Jesus through you. The journey has been about the *passion* of God becoming real to you so that the *Presence* of God can be seen through your life. This is your ultimate *purpose* in God.

Take time to reflect now on the *passion*, *Presence*, and the *purpose* of God in your life.

RESPOND

How will I make this visible through my life today?

(Now go to the reflection final section and gather all the manna along the way of your journey through this devotional.)

YOUR JOURNEY CONTINUES...

Each of the 90 devotionals of this book have been designed for your spiritual transformation. You began the journey reflecting with Don on the passion of God's love. In the second session you learned that the Presence of God surrounded you. Last, in the third section you discovered that God's ultimate purpose for you was sonship—to be an heir with Jesus Christ of the Kingdom of God, which is established in and flowing from you. Note that none of us have fully arrived at union with God perfectly. We have and will make missteps along the way, yet God continues to call us higher.

In this final section you are invited to reflect over the entire journey of this book. There is a little space for your reflections. I suggest you acquire an additional journal and continue your writing and reflections. Here are a few questions to guide but not limit your continuing journaling. This is not a quiz or a test, but a way to focus on areas for further growth in your relationship with God through Jesus Christ.

1. What kinds of words or images stood out to you in the devotional articles and Scriptures?

....

....

....

2. Which section was the most meaningful for you—
   the *passion* of God, the *Presence* of God, or the *purpose* in God? Why?

....

....

....

....

....

3. What touched you the most throughout the journey
   through this devotional?

....

....

....

....

....

4. What are you the most grateful for through your
   journey through this devotional?

....

....

....

....

5. What do you sense the Spirit of God saying to you
   through this devotional about His *passion*, *Presence*,
   and *purpose* for you?

....

....

....

....

6. Who might you invite to experience this devotional
   journey with you?

....

....

....

....

ABOUT DON NORI, SR.

Don Nori, Sr. passed into glory April 17, 2018, at the age of 66. He is survived by his wife, Cathy, their five sons, and seven grandchildren. Don was the founder of Destiny Image, Inc., a company dedicated to spreading the Word of God to the nations to inspire a godly generation. Through his own writings, and through publishing the writings of thousands more, Don leaves behind a legacy of leading believers the world over into a deeper relationship with Christ.

ABOUT THOM GARDNER

Thom Gardner has ministered as a Bible teacher or pastor since 1986, and is now President of Restored Life Ministries, Inc., a ministry dedicated to integrated spiritual formation. Dr. Gardner travels internationally to equip leaders throughout the body of Christ by leading retreats and training seminars using his techniques of interactive encounter of the Presence of Christ through the Scriptures. Dr. Gardner holds a Doctor of Ministry focused on Spiritual Formation from Winebrenner Theological Seminary, Findlay, Ohio. He has also served as an adjunct professor of Spiritual Formation at Winebrenner Seminary.

RESOURCES

Seminars:

- Life Equipping Seminar
- Rewriting Your Life Sentence
- Grace at the Table, Marriage Encounters
- Seven Things to tell Your Children

- Living the God-Breathed Life
- Make Up Your Mind/Moving from Decision to Discernment
- Everything That Grows

Books

Healing the Wounded Heart

The Healing Journey

Relentless Love

Living the God-Breathed Life

Everything that Grows

Growing Up Into Christ

E Course

Grace at the Table, Overcoming Obstacles in Relationship through Compassion